Fighting Colors

HAWKER HUI

in Color

by Robbie Robinson
illustrated by Robbie Robinson

squadron/signal publications

ACKNOWLEDGMENTS
I am very grateful to all who have been so kind in providing me with information
and photographs for this publication. Particularly C. Burbridge, Wing Commander H. Irving, P. Rowlings, Marshall of Cambridge, RAF Museum (Hen-
don), RAF Museum (Duxford), RAF (Mod.), No 1, 3, 41, 54 and 63 Squadrons.

If you have any photographs of the aircraft, armor, soldiers or ships of any
nation, particularly wartime snapshots, why not share them with us and help
make Squadron/Signal's books all the more interesting and complete in the
future. Any photograph sent to us will be copied and the original returned. The
donor will be fully credited for any photos used. Please send them to: Squadron/
Signal Publications, Inc., 1115 Crowley Dr., Carrollton, TX 75011-5010.

NOTE
The serial numbers accompanying the squadron histories are of aircraft known
to have served with that particular Squadron and are not an indication of Squadron strength. Individual code letters were sometimes moved from one aircraft to
another within a squadron, and sometimes aircraft were moved from one squadron to another. An aircraft letter was often duplicated, being seen on different
aircraft at different dates.

THE HAWKER HUNTER

The Hunter was undoubtedly one of the most beautiful aircraft to have served with the Royal Air Force. It served with the majority of Fighter Command Squadrons, at home in the United Kingdom, with the Second Tactical Air Force in Germany, and in the Near and Far East.

The Hunter was designed and directed by Sir Sidney Camm in 1948 as a replacement for the Gloster Meteor. There were several prototype aircraft undergoing tests and experiments, however, the most remembered was the Scarlet prototype flown by Squadron Leader Neville Duke. This aircraft, Hawker P1067 was the first prototype and had originally been painted in overall Light Green. It made its first flight on 20 July 1951 and was serialed WB 188. This prototype was later updated to F Mk 3 standards and re-engined with a Rolls-Royce Avon RA7R, with a special reheat to enable the Hunter to engage in attacks on the world speed records. With Squadron Leader Neville Duke at the controls, the aircraft was flown over a 3 kilometre course off the south coast of Rustington, establishing a new world speed record of 727.63 mph on 7 September 1953.

The second prototype, WB195, also powered with the Avon engine, was armed with four 30MM Aden Cannons, would serve as the basis of the production Hunter F Mk 1. On 16 May 1953 the initial production Hunter F Mk 1 (WT 555) flew for the first time at Dunsfold, although the Royal Air Force would not receive production deliveries for at least another year.

Fighter Command's other interceptor, the Supermarine Swift F Mk 1, had entered service with No 56 Squadron at RAF Waterbeach in February of 1954. However, it did not live up to expectations and encountered severe problems which caused several fatal accidents. The situation did not improve with the introduction of the Swift F Mk 2 variant into the squadron. All Swift fighters were withdrawn from service. However, Swift FR Mk 5s were used in the Reconnaissance role and served with the Second Tactical Air Force in Germany.

In July of 1954 the first Hunter F Mk 1s, powered by Rolls Royce Avon 104 and 107 engines, and built by Hawker Aircraft, Kingston-upon-Thames Division, began to enter service with No 43 Squadron at RAF Leuhars, Scotland. By this time the Hunter F Mk 2, powered by the Armstrong-Siddeley Sapphire 101 engine was flying, and by November of 1954 the F Mk 2 began entering service with No 257 Squadron based at RAF Wattisham in Suffolk.

These early Hunters were not without problems, and like the Swifts they also had a number of fatalities, however, the F Mk 2 variant suffered fewer problems than the F Mk 1. The problem of endurance with the aircraft flying for only 35-40 minutes was paramount. In spite of these early problems the Hunter proved to be a first class aircraft and operational squadrons quickly began forming Aerobatic teams.

The Royal Air Force continued pressing the Hunter into service, with it eventually becoming the backbone of Fighter Command. With the F Mk 4 variant, powered by the Avon 113 or 115, being introduced into service, the earlier F Mk 1s were gradually distributed among second line units such as the Central Fighter Establishment's Operational Conversion Units (OCUs) and the Fighter Weapons School. No 98 Squadron of the Second Tactical Air Force (Germany) was first to receive the F Mk 4, and was quickly followed by No 112 Squadron, and then the Hunter being distributed to home based Squadrons.

The next variant was the Sapphire engined Hunter F Mk 5 which entered service in March of 1955. First to receive this version was No 263 Squadron at RAF Wattisham, which had previously operated the F Mk 2. Next was No 56 Squadron replacing its unsuccessful Swifts, followed by No 1 and 41 Squadrons and eventually No 34 Squadron who flew sixteen of their aircraft to Cyprus during the Suez crisis in 1956.

With the success of the Hunter F Mk 4 and F Mk 5, the Hunter F Mk 6, to be powered by the larger and more powerful Rolls-Royce Avon 203/207 engine, was already being considered. A few initial problems arose but these were quickly remedied, and in May of 1956 deliveries commenced to No 19 Squadron, making them the first unit to operate the Hunter F Mk 6, followed by 63, 111 and 43 Squadrons. Treble-one Squadron soon formed an Aerobatic Team which became world famous, and was followed by No 92's Blue Diamonds.

Like the Vampire and Meteor Fighters which had trainer versions there was also need of a trainer Hunter, and so the trainer Hunter T Mk 7 was soon under development. These Hunter trainers had side by side seating, and a compartment was built into the rear of the fuselage housing a parachute. Each of the Fighter Command Squadrons was to receive at least one T Mk 7 trainers, with a number of others going to No 229 Operational Conversion Unit (OCU) in 1958.

For some time the F Mk 6 had been undergoing tests to see if the Hawker Hunter was suitable for the ground attack role. Various underwing loads were tested, including 100 and 230 gallon drop tanks, 1000 and 500 pound bombs, practice bombs, rockets, Firestreak and Fireflash missiles. These experiments led up to a new aircraft variant known as the ground attack Hunter FGA Mk 9 variant. The first Hunter FGA Mk 9s were

(Above) Hawker Hunter FGA Mk 9, XG130 (E), of No 1 Squadron carrying a full compliment of Drop Tanks at RAF West Raynham in 1965. The squadron emblem is flanked by White pennants outlined in Red, and the wingtips are White. (Map)

interim ground attack aircraft, powered by the earlier Avon 203s. Later in 1959, with the installation of the Avon 207 engine in converted F Mk 6 airframes, the definitive Hunter FGA Mk 9 ground attack variant was delivered. Conversions of Hunter F Mk 6 fighters to Hunter FGA Mk 9 standards continued into the mid 1960's as the English Electric Lightning was coming into service and taking over the interceptor role.

With Fighter Command terminating in April of 1958, Strike Command was formed, with the role remaining the same. From June of 1965 most of the FGA Mk 9 equipped Squadrons were to see service overseas being employed in the policing role, such as No 8, 43, and 208 Squadrons of the Aden Strike Wing at Khormaksar. The Far East Air Force had No 20 Squadron at Tengah and 28 Squadron at Kai-Tak, Hong Kong while the United Kingdom based Units were No 1 and 54 Squadrons.

With the Swift FRS due to be retired from service in 1961, The Royal Air Force was interested in employing the Hunter in the Fighter Reconnaissance role as a replacement aircraft for the Swift. Hunter F Mk 4 WT780 had conducted trials with five cameras fitted to the nose, and Hunter F Mk 6 XF429 was tested with three nose cameras from late 1958. The resulting reconnaissance aircraft was designated the Hunter FR Mk 10 embodying all the modifications of the FGA MK 9 retained the four 30MM Aden cannons and the three nose cameras.

Late in 1960 Hunter FR Mk 10 aircraft were delivered to the Second Tactical Airforce, with 2 and 4 Squadrons receiving them first, they also went to 1417 Flight of No 8 Squadron at Khormaksar and 229 OCU at RAF Chivenor.

COLOR SCHEMES

When the Hunter first entered service they retained the overall Silver paint scheme, however, camouflage was soon introduced consisting of Dark Green and Dark Sea Grey upper surfaces over Silver under surfaces.

This *standard* scheme was applied to all Fighter Command, including the Second Tactical Air Force Squadrons based in Germany. However some of the Hunters based in Germany initially carried the earlier Second Tactical Air Force scheme consisting of the standard camouflage on the upper surfaces with PR Blue on the under surfaces. 118 Squadron had an aircraft in this scheme and one or two were seen at 229 OCU RAF Chivenor during the late 1950s. From mid 1966 the Silver undersides were replaced by a Light Aircraft Grey on the undersides of the standard scheme.

Initially Hunter T Mk 7 trainers were overall Silver with Yellow training bands on the wings and fuselage, but by the mid 1960s the Yellow areas were being replaced by Dayglo Orange bands, although the application varied from unit to unit, with some having the Day-glo applied to the nose and wing tips. By 1971 the standard camouflage was being applied to the T Mk 7 although Squadrons in the Middle and Far East had carried it from the onset.

NO 1 SQUADRON

No 1 Squadron was formed in April of 1912 within the Royal Flying Corps. It was originally a Balloon Unit but became a Flying unit equipped with the Nieuport 17 cl when it moved to Brooklands in 1914 and them to France in 1916. The squadron re-equipped with SE5As during early 1918 and saw extensive action against the Germans. Returning to United Kingdom the squadron was disbanded during January of 1920 and reformed the same month.

No 1 Squadron moved to India, operating Nieuports and Sopwith Snipes, tasked with Policing duties. It disbanded again in 1926, but was reformed in February of 1927 at RAF Tangmere, Sussex, which would be its home for many years. It was equipped with the Siskin IIIa until 1932, and with the Hawker Fury from 1932 until 1938.

At the outbreak of World War II, the Squadron was equipped with Hurricanes gradually re-equipping with later marks of the Hurricane as the war progressed. Beginning in 1942 the Typhoon served with the unit for two years, before being replaced by the Spitfire Mk IX and later the Mk 21. The Squadron entered the jet era late in 1946, being equipped with Gloster Meteor F Mk 3s, then the F Mk 4, and finally the F Mk 8 variant in 1950 which saw service until September of 1955.

During 1954, Flight Lieutenant H Irving of No 1 Squadron became the Solo Aerobatic Display Pilot for the 1955/56 season flying a Hunter F Mk 5, WP146, after completing a Hunter conversion course at RAF Chivenor.

No 1 Squadron received its first Hunter F Mk 2 (WN919), for conversion purposes in early 1955, with the first Hunter F Mk 5s arriving in June of 1955. Flight Lieutenant Irving personally converted all No 1 Squadron pilots to the type.

The Red and White rectangular markings used on No 1 Squadron's Meteor F Mk 8s were perpetuated on the nose of the Hunters in the form of two Red and White pennants flanking the Squadron emblem on a White circular field with a Red border. Individual aircraft letters in Red were on the tail outlined in White, and repeated in Black on the nosewheel doors.

During the Suez crisis in 1956, a proving flight was flown from Tangmere to Cyprus. On 4 May Flight Lieutenant Irving flew Hunter WN959, accompanied by three other aircraft and pilots: Wing Commander P.J. Simpson, Squadron Leader F.W. Lister, and Flight Lieutenant D.T. Bryant. The four aircraft landed at Istres in Southern France, Luqa in Malta, El Adem in Libya and Nicosia on Cyprus on 5th May. Total flying time was 5 hours 10 minutes.

OPERATION QUICKFIRE

On 7 August 1956 the Tangmere Wing, equipped with a modified Hunter F Mk 5 (Sapphire type 10101 engines), flew to Cyprus, via Istres, Luqa and El Adem to re-inforce the Middle East Air Force. The force consisted of two Operational Squadrons (No 1 and 34), and two supporting Squadrons of personnel. The force was commanded by Wing Commander P.J. Simpson, DSO, DFC, with No 1 Squadron being commanded by Flight Lieutenant Irving and No 34 Squadron under the command of Squadron Leader A.F. Wilson, DFC. Twenty-five aircraft left Tangmere in six flights of four, with all aircraft completing the flight of over 2,000 miles to Akrotiri in under five hours flying time.

To this Hunter equipped wing was vested the responsibility of defending the main Middle East bases in Cyprus. Exercises in this role were carried out from Akrotiri and later from Nicosia beginning on 1 September 1956.

With the outbreak of war between Israel and Egypt at the end of October, the Wing stood at readiness from dawn to dusk. With the intervention of British and French Forces into the hostilities, fighter sweeps by the Wing penetrated into Egypt as far as Cairo, and on 2 November Canberras were escorted on bombing and photographic missions over Egypt. On 5 November, relays of four Hunter aircraft provided top cover for transport aircraft ferrying paratroopers during Airborne Operations at Gamil airfield.

During the Suez operations the Hunters retained the Squadron nose markings, but were much larger on the F Mk 5 aircraft than on later variants operated by the Squadron. After arriving in Cyprus, additional markings were applied in the form of Black and Yellow identification bands. These bands were three alternating one foot wide Yellow and two one foot Black bands painted around the wings and rear fuselage, although there may well have been slight variations in the positioning of the bands. Some aircraft are believed to have received only Yellow paint.

The Hunter F Mk 5s served with No 1 Squadron until it was disbanded in June of 1958. It reformed again in July of 1958 from No 263 Squadron and was based at RAF Stradishall and equipped with the Hunter F Mk 6 variant with which it was to operate until 1961. The squadron markings were slightly smaller on the F Mk 6 with a Red aircraft letter on the nosewheel door instead of the earlier Black letter.

Late in 1961 the squadron moved to RAF Waterbeach, Cambridgeshire, and was re-equipped with the FGA Mk 9 ground attack Hunter. In August of 1963 the squadron moved to RAF West Raynham, and remained there until July of 1959 during which time the squadron markings continued to be carried on the aircraft in the same manner as carried on the earlier F Mk 6, with the exception of the code letters which now became White on the tail and Black on the nosewheel door.

Aircraft known to have been on strength with No 1 Squadron
F Mk 5 - WN988 (A), WP113 (Q), WP119 (T), WP121 (W), WP147 (G)

F Mk 5s of No 1 Squadron known to have been involved in Suez operations
WN973 (B), WN975 (C), WN977 (P), WP105 (R), WP121 (W)
WP137 (S), WP138 (T), WP147 (G), WP188 (X), WP190 (K)
WP191 (Z), **F Mk 6 -** XE624 (B), XG207 (F), XE628 (X)
FGA Mk 9 - XG130 (E), XE591 (H), XE646 (V)

(Above) FR Mk 10, XE605 (O), of No 2 Squadron at Norvenich Air Base, Germany during 1970. The rectangles on either side of the roundel are Black with White triangles, and the White triangle on the tail has the aircraft letter in Black. (Map)

NO 2 SQUADRON

In May of 1912 No 2 Squadron was formed as a reconnaissance unit. Commencing reconnaissance duties in World War I in co-operation with the Army, No 2 Squadron flew aircraft such as the Armstrong Whitworth FK 8. During World War II it operated aircraft such as Lysanders, Mustangs, and Spitfires in the Photo Reconnaissance role.

In 1953 the squadron was based at Wahn, West Germany, operating Meteor FR Mk 9s as part of the 2nd Tactical Air Force. Based at RAF Geilenkirchen in 1956 the squadron operated the Swift FR Mk 5, which in turn was replaced by the Hunter FR Mk 10 durng 1961.

The unit, transferred to Gutersloh, flying the Hunter FR Mk 10 until 1969, during which time the markings consisted of Black rectangles on each side of the fuselage roundel, with a White triangle in each Black rectangle. An individual aircraft letter was carried on a Black or White tail triangle. A White letter painted on a Black nosewheel door. The Hunter remained with the Squadron until January of 1971 when re-equipment with the Phantom FGR 2 began.

Hawker Hunters known to be on strength with No 2 Squadron
FR Mk 10 - WW586 (N), XE625 (I), XE605 (O), WV372 (R)
T Mk 7 - XF457 (T), XF458 (W)

(Above)Hunter T Mk 7 two seat trainer, WV372 (R), of 2 Squadron at RAF Wildenrath's open day in July of 1970.

NO 3 SQUADRON

No 3 Squadron traces its history back to 1909/1910 when various experiments in heavier-than-air flights were carried out by private individuals working with the Royal Engineers Balloon factory on Salisbury Plain. In September of 1910 two Bristol Boxkite machines took part in army maneuvers for the first time, and they were so successful that eventually an Air Battalion of The Royal Engineers was formed. The Battalion, made up of three companies, had its headquarters and a company at Farnborough, a company at Larkhill, and another at Brooklands. The Air Battalion had a short existence, with its successor, The Royal Flying Corps (RFC) coming into being on 13 April 1912, with No 2 Company becoming No 3 Squadron of the RFC. Consequently No 3 Squadron can rightful claim to being the oldest British aircraft unit, descending directly from No 2 Company of the Air Battalion.

At the outbreak of the First World War, No 3 Squadron was the first British flying unit to arrive in France during August of 1914, and was equipped with the Sopwith Camel F.1., which it flew until February of 1919 when the Squadron returned home to disband.

Reforming, the squadron spent the inter-war years flying the Walrus as a General Reconnaissance and Fleet Support unit, but disbanding again, and reforming again in 1924 with Sopwith Snipes.

During World War II, the Hurricane was on strength until February of 1943, when the it was replaced by Typhoon 16s at Hunsden. After VE Day No 3 Squadron had periods of duty at various German bases, including Berlin, before being re-equipped with Vampires and moving to Gutersloh in 1948. In 1952 they moved to Wildenrath and during the spring of 1953 the conversion to Sabre F Mk 1s began. These sweptwing fighters carried Light Green intakes and later had Light Green rectangles painted on each side of the fuselage roundels. Individual aircraft letters were Red with White outlines.

The Squadron took its Sabres to Geilenkirchen and in May of 1956 began to equip with the Hunter F Mk 4. Like its earlier Sabres, the Hunters also carried Green rectangles flanking the roundels with individual aircraft tail letters in Red with White outlines. The Hunter served with No 3 Squadron until June of 1957, when it was replaced by the Javelin FAW Mk 4.

Hunter aircraft known to have been on strength with No 3 Squadron
F Mk 4 - XF944 ( ), XF949 (C), XF968 (R), XF975 (W), XF990 (K)

(Above) F Mk 4, WV275 (D), of No 4 Squadron based at Jever under the 2nd Tactical Air Force, in 1954. The squadron burst on the nose had a 4 centered in it and a lightning bolt running diagonally across it. (Map)

NO 4 SQUADRON

Formed during the autumn of 1912, No 4 Squadron like No 2 Squadron, was also assigned to the reconnaissance role, operating aircraft such as the R.E.8 during World War I, and Lysanders during World War II.

The role of the Squadron changed in 1950 when it became a Fighter Squadron based at Wunstorf in Germany flying Vampire FB Mk 5s. The Squadron moved to Jever in 1953 and re-equipped with the Sabre F Mk 4, operating this aircraft until 1956 when the Sabre was superseded by the Hunter F Mk 4. The rectangular markings previously carried on the Sabre were perpetuated on the fuselage sides of the Hunter, while the figure 4 and Squadron emblem were placed on the sides of the nose.

In 1957 the F Mk 4 was replaced by the Hunter F Mk 6 Variant and the markings were reduced in size and moved onto the nose, flanking the Squadron emblem. White code letters remained on the tail with Black letters on Silver nosewheel doors. In 1961 the Squadron reverted to the fighter/reconnaissance role, flying the Swift FR Mk 5 for a short period.

Late in 1961 the Squadron re-equipped with the Hunter FR Mk 10 at RAF Gutersloh. No 4 Squadron markings were one of the most colorful units. The rectangular fuselage markings were raised slightly, bringing them level with the top of the roundel. The markings were also carried on the sides of the nose in a slightly smaller scale. White code letters were carried on the tail and repeated on Red nose wheel doors. The Hunter served with the squadron until 1970, when it was replaced by the Harrier.

Hawker Hunters known to be on strength with No 4 Squadron
F Mk 4 — WV275 (D), WV321 (B), WV226 (V), WT799 ( )
F Mk 6 — XG263 ( ), XG270 ( ), XE590 (V)
FR Mk 10 — XF459 (F), XE580 (D), XE585 (A), XJ714 (J), WW595 (G)

(Above) FGA Mk 9 ground attack Hunter, XJ689 (B), of No 8 Squadron at Khormaksar in 1966/67. The tri-color rectangles have been raised level with the top of the roundel. (Map)

(Above) F Mk 6, XJ646 (D), of No 14 Squadron at Wethersfield, Essex in 1962 carrying the squadron's White rectangles with Blue diamonds level with the top of the roundel. Gun blast deflectors have been added, this was a modification made to some F Mk 6 and FGA Mk 9 Hunters. (Map)

NO 8 SQUADRON

After being formed in 1915 No 8 Squadron took on the role of policing and was posted to Aden in 1927. The aircraft flown at this time was the D.H.9A Vickers Vincent and eventually the Bristol Blenheim. The Blenheims were in use when the Squadron's role changed to that of maritime patrol and Wellingtons were assigned to the Squadron. Later the Liberator was used in the Far East where the Squadron performed as a Special Duties Squadron.

The Squadron again took up the policing duty when it was posted to Khormaksar in Aden during 1947, where it flew Tempests in the ground attack role. For a short time it operated Bristol Brigands. In 1952 No 8 was equipped with the Vampire FB Mk 9 and during the following years it also operated the Venom FB Mk 1 and Mk 4.

Early in 1960, while still based at RAF Khormaksar, the squadron began to re-equip with the faster and more up to date Hunter FGA Mk 9. The unit's tri-colored rectangular markings were applied to the fuselage sides, and a White aircraft letter was painted on the Red nose wheel door. Later the squadron carried a bright Red sheathed Arabian dagger painted on a Silver backing. The individual tail code letter remained White.

In 1963 No 43 Squadron, also equipped with Hunter FGA Mk 9s, carrying 43 Squadron's customary Black and White checkerboard markings, was transferred to Khormaksar. No 43 Squadron was absorbed into No 8 Squadron before being disbanded in October of 1967. After absorbing No 43 Squadron's checkerboard markings were added to No 8 Squadron's aircraft, with all aircraft now carried the triple colors of No 8 Squadron on one side of the roundel and the Black and White checkers of No 43 Squadron on the other side. The tail letter remained White and was repeated in Black on the nose wheel door. The Squadron moved to the Persian Gulf, where it remained until disbanding in 1971.

Hawker Hunters known to have been on strength with No 8 Squadron

FGA Mk 9 - 8 Squadron Markings
XF655 (H), XJ689 (B), XG128 (Q), XG256 (H), XJ646 (H)

FGA Mk 9 - 8 and 43 Squadron markings
XG298 (J), XJ646 (P), XE552 (D), XE550 (X), XE645 (SW)

(Above) T Mk 7, XF321 (TZ), carrying the Black and White checkers of No 43 Squadron and the tri-color markings of No 8 squadron on either side of the fuselage roundel, and No 1417 Reconnaissance Flight arrowhead on the nose, Khormaksar 1966/67. (Map)

1417 FLIGHT

No 8 Squadron operated a number of reconnaissance Meteor FR Mk 9s alongside of their Venoms. These reconnaissance Meteors retained their four cannon armament with cameras being mounted in the forward nose section. When the Squadron received the Hunter, a number of Hunter FR Mk 10 variants were assigned to undertake the fighter reconnaissance role at RAF Khormaksar and during 1961 No 1417 Flight was formed.

Hunters of No 1417 Flight carried their own colors which comprised an arrow head design of Black, Blue, Yellow and Green. A White circular field containing the Station crest was super-imposed on the arrow. Individual code letters were not carried on these aircraft, but instead the pilots initials in either White or Yellow on the tail, and were repeated in Light Blue on the nose wheel door. 1417 Flight remained at Khormaksar with 8 Squadron until disbanding in 1971.

Hawker Hunters known to be on strength with No 1417 Flight
FR Mk 10 - XF441 (FG), XE614 (GC), XF460 (GT), XE589 (JM), XE589 (RC)
Commanding Officers's aircraft - XF460 (RB), XF429 (KS)

No 14 SQUADRON

No 14 Squadron formed on 3 February 1915 and spent most of its time overseas. The unit became an Army co-operation Squadron in Palestine, and later became a Bomber Squadron. It became a Coastal Squadron flying Marauders up to 1945, however, in 1950 it became a Fighter/Bomber Squadron flying Mosquitos and Vampires at Celle Germany with 2nd Tactical Air Force.

In 1955 the Hunter Mk F Mk 4 replaced the Vampires at Oldenberg. No 14 Squadron Hunters carried White rectangles containing three Blue diamonds applied to each side of the fuselage. However, since these fuselage markings were prone to streaking and scarring, with the introduction of the Hunter F Mk 6 variant to the Squadron in April of 1957, the fuselage markings were raised to a point level with the top of the roundel.

Individual aircraft letters varied somewhat with a White on Black circle and Black on a White circle. The letter was repeated in Black on the nosewheel door and in a large format with a White band and Blue diamonds below. The Hunter last operated at Gutersloh in 1962 when the Squadron disbanded on 17 December 1962.

Hawker Hunters known to be on strength with No 14 Squadron
F Mk 4 - WW663 (H), WT711(A), XE657(Y)
F Mk 6 - XJ712 (B), XJ646 (D), XJ689(F), XG274 (P), XG251 (E), XK149 (T)

(Above) F Mk 6, XG133 (A), of 19 Squadron. This aircraft has yet to receive the 'Sawtooth' wing leading edge modification, which was fitted to late production aircraft, and retro-fitted to earlier batches. White wing tips with Blue lightning bolts are carried. (Map)

NO 19 SQUADRON

The actual date of forming is unknown, however, the squadron is known to have been flying the B.E.12 Fighter in 1916. It went on to fly other early types such as the Spad VII and in April of 1923 was flying the Gloster Grebe.

During the World War II years, the Spitfire Mk 1 was being operated in 1940 and the RAF's Mustang III and IV during 1944/1945. The first Jet Fighters to be operated by the Squadron was the Gloster Meteor F Mk 8s at RAF Church Fenton, between 1951 and 1957. The Hunter F Mk 6 joined the Squadron in late 1956 and carried the traditional 19 Squadron Blue and White checkered markings. Wing tips were also painted, with one aircraft, XG152 (X), having the port wing tip painted Blue and the starboard wing tip being painted White. Yellow individual aircraft letters were carried on the tail. These markings eventually gave way to the more standard markings of White wing tips with Blue lightning bolts.

However, with the introduction of White serial numbers in 1959/60 some of 19 Squadron's aircraft carried White tail letters. The unit moved to RAF Leconfield in 1959, continuing to fly the Hunter until early 1963 when it was replaced by the Lightning F Mk 2.

Hawker Hunters known to be on strength with No 19 Squadron
F Mk 6 - XF449 (S), XG152 (X), XG135 (G), XG133 (A), XG191 (G), XE561 (Z), XG169 (Q), XG191 (E), XF527 (P)

(Above) FGA Mk 9, XF437 (V) of 20 Squadron in immaculate condition at Tengah Singapore. The squadron eagle is set in a White circle. (Map).

No 20 SQUADRON

Formed on 1 September 1915 as a Fighter unit, No 20 Squadron first flew the F.E.2B, and later the Bristol F.2B. The Squadron mainly served overseas between 1916 and 1919. It went on to operate the Hurricane in various marks from 1943 to 1945, and Spitfire Mk 8s and FR Mk 14s during the post war period.

No 20 Squadron joined the 2nd Tactical Air Force in 1952 with a posting to Oldenburg, and began operations with the Vampire FB Mk 9. The Vampire was replaced by the Sabre F Mk 1 in 1954. Squadron markings were Blue rectangles with Red, White and Green bars on each side of the fuselage roundels, the squadron Eagle emblem on a White circle was painted on the Sabre's nose.

In 1955 the Hunter F Mk 4 came on to the scene and like the Sabre, carried the squadron markings flanking the roundel. The Squadron moved to Gutersloh in 1957 where the Hunter F Mk 6 was taken on strength, and carried the same markings.

The squadron disbanded in 1960 but reformed again with the Far East Force at Tengah, Singapore. This time it took on the ground attack role and equipped with the Hunter FGA Mk 9. The rectangular squadron markings were moved to the aircraft's nose flanking the Eagle emblem set on a White circle. The nose wheel doors were painted Red with XX on the top portion and the aircraft letter below, these and the tail letters were White with Light Blue trim. Later, the nose wheel door markings changed to incorporate a large aircraft letter. The Hunter remained with No 20 Squadron until it disbanded at Tengah in February of 1970.

Hawker Hunters known to be on strength with No 20 Squadron
F Mk 4 - WV395 (W), WV401 (T), WV410 (X)
F Mk 6 - XG128 (Y), XK138 (M), XE610 (C)
FGA 9 - XF437 (V), XF414 (E), XF310 (T)

(Above) F Mk 4, WV410 (B), of No 26 Squadron at RAF Benson's Battle of Britain display on 4 September 1957. A springbok's head is carried on a White disc flanked by Black rectangles outlined in Green with Green lightning bolts inset in the rectangles. (Map)

No 26 SQUADRON

No 26 Squadron was formed during October of 1915, but after only two years it disbanded. When it reformed in 1937, it operated the Lysander on Army cooperation duties. Later in World War II it operated Spitfires and Mustangs in the Reconnaissance Role.

After the war, the Squadron was again disbanded, reforming in 1946 from No 41 Squadron, flying the reconnaissance Spitfire PR Mk 11 and FR Mk 14. Transferring to the 2nd Tactical Air Force, the squadron was based at Gutersloh in 1947 flying the Tempest F Mk 2. The Tempest was replaced by the Vampire in 1949 and served with the Squadron until November of 1953. Still part of the 2nd Tactical Air Force, No 26 Squadron moved to Oldenburg in August of 1953 where it re-equipped with the Sabre F Mk 1 and was assigned to the Interceptor role. The Sabres carried a Springbok emblem on a White disc high on the aircraft's tail. Individual aircraft letters in White were carried next to the fuselage roundel.

In June of 1955 when the Hawker Hunter F Mk 4 began replacing the Sabre, the markings were changed with the Springbok emblem being moved to the nose and flanked with small Green and Black rectangles. Yellow aircraft code letters were painted on the tail.

In September of 1957 the Squadron was disbanded, but was reformed at RAF Gutersloh in 1958 and equipped with the Hunter F Mk 6. The markings on the F Mk 6 remained the same as those on the F Mk 4 variant except for being considerably enlarged. The color of the nosewheel door code letter is uncertain, however, XF415 (J) and XJ717 (Z) carried markings depicted in the color illustrations. The Hunter served with the Squadron until it disbanded in 1961.

Hawker Hunters known to be on strength with No 26 Squadron
F Mk 4 - WT722 (S), WT769 (B), WW664 (C), XE668 (G)
F Mk 6 - XE530 (A), XF535 (F), XF415 (J), XJ636 (E)

(Above) Hunter FGA Mk 9, XG297 (B), of No 28 Squadron with Yellow wing tips. Squadron markings are Blue rectangles with Yellow outlines flanking a White disc containing a flying Pegasus. (Map)

No 28 SQUADRON

No 28 Squadron was formed in November of 1915 from a nucleus of South African pilots and spent the its early years as a training unit, but took on the Fighter role in 1917 when it was equipped with the Sopwith F1 Camel.

The Squadron spent most of the immediate post-war period moving about Italy and finally disbanded at Eastleigh during 1920. After reforming as No 114 Squadron during the same year, they received Bristol Fighters and later Audaxes. The Audax entered World War II with No 28 Squadron but gave way to the Lysander. In December of 1942 the Hurricane was used for reconnaissance duties with the Army in Burma.

In 1949 No 28 came under the Far East Air Force when it moved to Kai Tak, Hong Kong. Once there, the Spitfire FR Mk 18 was on strength until 1951 when the Vampire FR Mk 5 joined the Squadron and it again became a Fighter squadron. The Vampires served until 1956, when Venoms replaced them. During this period No 28 Squadron aircraft carried Blue and Yellow rectangles on the aircraft's booms, with the Venoms also having Yellow wingtip tanks with a Blue lightning streak.

In 1962 the squadron began to receive Hawker Hunter FGA Mk 9s. The squadron markings were applied to the aircraft's nose and were still comprised of Blue and Yellow rectangles which flanked the Pegasus emblem in the center. Code letters were White on the tail and repeated in Black on the nosewheel door. The Hunter served with No 28 until it disbanded in 1967.

Hawker Hunters known to be on strength with No 28 Squadron
FGA Mk 9 - XE622 (A), XG291 (C), WV389 (T)
T7 - XE535 (C)

(Above) F Mk 5, WP112(E), of No 34 Squadron being refuelled. A huge aircraft letter is carried on the nosewheel door, which is not so unusual when it is considered that the squadron insignia was perhaps the largest carried on a Hunter.

No 34 SQUADRON

This Squadron was formed on 7 January 1916 and served as an Army co-operation Squadron in France and later on the Italian front. It returned to the UK in 1919, disbanding later that year.

The squadron reformed in 1935 as a light Bomber Squadron operating Blenheim Mk 1's in Singapore. The Blenheim served with the unit until 1943 when the Squadron changed from Bomber to the Fighter role and began operating Hawker Hurricanes. With the Hurricane No 34 Squadron flew fighter escort for bombing raids and strafed targets at low level. For a short time the Squadron flew the Thunderbolt Mk II before disbanding in 1945.

In July of 1954 the Squadron entered the jet age when it reformed as a Fighter Squadron at RAF Tangmere on the Meteor F Mk 8. At this stage the markings were rather sparse with the squadron emblem on a very small White disc carried on the engine nacelles. The Meteor served with the squadron until August of 1956 when the unit was re-equipped with the Hunter F Mk 5. The Squadron markings applied to the sides of the nose may have been the largest in Fighter Command, covering nearly the full length of the front fuselage. Yellow individual aircraft letters were painted on the tail and repeated in White or Yellow on a Black nosewheel door.

Late in 1956 34 Squadron sent Hunters to Nicosia, Cyprus in support of the Suez operations where the aircraft had Black and Yellow identification markings painted around the wings and fuselage. No 34 Squadron's deployment was brief and they returned to Tangmere in December of 1956, where they remained until disbanding on 10 January 1958.

Hawker Hunters known to be on strength with No 34 Squadron
F M 5 - WN970 (L), WP126 (R), WP184 (A), WP144 (X), WP133 (L),
WP111 (M), WP113 (V), WP130 (S), WP140 (R), WP142 (W), WP185 (E),
F Mk 5s involved in Suez Operations
WN978 (B), WP182 (C), WP139 (J), WP136 (N), WP140 (R),
WP130 (S) WP132 (T), WP113 (V)

(Above) F Mk 5, WP148 (K), of No 41 Squadron at RAF Biggin Hill, which was 41's home while flying the Hawker Hunter. The Loraine Cross squadron insignia was in recognition of the squadron's base at St Omer in France during World War I. (Map)

No 41 SQUADRON

Formed in 1916, No 41 Squadron took part in battles over the Somme flying aircraft such as the F.E.8 in ground attack work, and later the D.H.5 in the same role. After the war the squadron returned to the UK and disbanded in 1919.

Reforming in 1923 No 41 operated the Sopwith Snipe, followed by the Siskin, Bristol Bulldog, Hawker Demon, and finally the Hawker Fury in 1937. In January of 1939, Spitfire Mk 1's were taken on strength and later Spitfire Mk IIs. Other Spitfires used were the Mk 12, Mk 14 and in April 1946 the Mk 21 was being flown.

In April of 1947 the Squadron was based at RAF Church Fenton flying the Hornet long range Fighter. It moved to RAF Biggin Hill in 1951 flying the Gloster Meteor F Mk 8. The camouflaged Meteor carried Red and White rectangles flanking the fuselage roundels with the Commanding Officers aircraft having a Red and White stripe on the leading edge of the tail.

In 1955 Meteors gave way to the Hawker Hunter F Mk 5. The Hunters carried a Red and White French Lorraine Cross (a link from the days when the Unit's Headquarters were at St Omer in France during 1916) on the nose flanked by Red and White bars. The aircraft letter was Red outlined in White, and was repeated on the nosewheel door in Red with a Red Lorraine Cross above it. One F Mk 5 aircraft had the tail painted White with the initials 'PT' on it, and repeated on nosewheel door. The Hunter served with the Squadron until early 1958, when it was replaced by the Gloster Javelin.

Hawker Hunters known to be on strength with No 41 Squadron
F Mk 5 - WP122 (A), WP148 (K), WN965 (P), WP187 (R), WP186 (PT),
WN967 (A), WP141 (B), WN964 (C), WP133 (D), WN963 (F)
WN956 (G), WP123 (O)

No 43 SQUADRON

Formed in April of 1916, No 43 Squadron started off flying the Sopwith Camel in 1917, then the Sopwith Snipe, and the Gloster Gamecock in 1926. As early as 1926 Black and White checkers were being applied to the fuselage sides and along the length of the upper wing surface of squadron aircraft.

During World War II the checkers of course disappeared, with the Hurricane and Spitfires being camouflaged and carrying the Squadron and aircraft code letters along the fuselage sides. However, the checkers reappeared again at the end of the war on the tails of Spitfire Mk 9s.

For a short time the Meteor F Mk 4 joined the Squadron in 1949, being replaced by the Meteor F Mk 8 in 1950. No 43 Squadron was based at RAF Leuchars, Scotland at this time, and in 1954 the Meteors began to be replaced by the Hunter F Mk 1. No 43 Squadron had the distinction of being the first Squadron to operate the Hunter. The Black and White checkered markings were applied to the fuselage sides, flanking the roundel. The individual aircraft letter was White and was carried at the rear of the fuselage sides. The nosewheel doors began to be painted Red with a White aircraft letter superimposed. A caricature of a Fighting Cock emblem was painted on the port side of the aircraft's nose.

In 1955, 43 Squadron formed an aerobatic team of four aircraft. The markings changed only slightly, with the checkers being raised to a point where they were level with the top of the roundels.

March of 1956 saw the unit re-equipping with the Hunter F Mk 4 variant with the checkers being raised on all aircraft, and the individual aircraft letters being painted on the tails. Checkered wing tips were also applied. The Unit continued with an Aerobatic Team and displayed at the SBAC Display at Farnborough in September of 1956.

The Hunter F Mk 4 served with the Squadron until 1957, but in December 1956 its replacement, the Hunter, F Mk 6 had begun to arrive. Markings were unchanged from those of the F Mk 4 version. The Squadron Commander's Aircraft, XE560 (G), lacked the Red and White nose wheel door, carrying instead a Squadron Leaders Flag with a Black '43' painted on a Silver nosewheel door.

The final Hunter variant to serve with the Squadron was the FGA Mk9, which replaced the F Mk 6 in 1960. At first the markings were the same as those found on the F Mk 6 but were later moved to the sides of the nose with the Squadron emblem in the center. The Squadron moved to Nicosia, Cyprus during the summer of 1961, where it remained until 1963 when it was posted to Khormaksar in Aden where it was disbanded in November of 1967.

Prior to this No 43 Squadron's markings had been taken over and incorporated onto No 8 Squadron's Hunter FGA Mk 9s. All aircraft carried both No 8 and No 43 Squadron markings on each side of the fuselage roundel.

Hunters known to be on strength with No 43 Squadron
F Mk 1 - WW599 (A), WT582 (B), WT587 (C), WT580 (E), WT565 (F), WT622 (G)
WT613 (R), WT581 (S), WW645 (S), WT618 (O), WT594 (N)
F Mk 4 - XE702 (B), XF982 (D), WV378 (H), XG341 (H), WV366 (T), XE663 (V),
WV324 (U)
F Mk 6 - XE560 (G), XE561 (D),XE615 (R), XF435 (P), XF456 (A), XF515 (R)
FGA Mk 9 - XG296 (A), XG237 (C), XJ684 (D), XE546 (B), XG292 (U), XK137 (P)

(Below) Precision flying Hunter F Mk 1s of No 43 Squadron show off the clean lines of these early aircraft. Black and White checker markings are carried on either side of the roundel. 1955 (RAF Mod.)

(Below) F Mk 6, XF515 (R), of 43 Squadron carrying fuselage checkers that have been raised to the top of the roundel. A strip of twenty-two Black and White checkers have been added to the wing tips, and a large White aircraft letter is carried on a Red nosewheel door. (Map)

(Below) FGA Mk 9, XJ646 (P), of 8/43 Squadron at Khormaksar in 1967 carrying both the checkers of 43 Squadron, which had been absorbed into No 8 Squadron during 1967, and the Yellow, Blue, Red tri-color markings of No 8 Squadron.

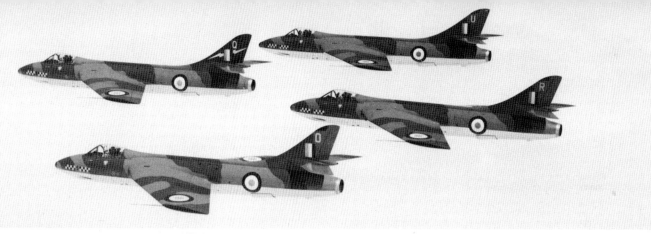

NO 45 SQUADRON.

No 45 Squadron had been formed on 1 March 1916, receiving its training in the UK before going to France in October of 1916. The Sopwith Camel was flown from mid-1917 until early 1919, when the unit returned to the UK and disbanded.

On the eve of World War II No 45 Squadron re-formed as a Bomber Squadron. It operated aircraft such as the Blenheim in 1939, receiving the Vultee Vengeance in 1942. Between 1944 and 1947, the DeHavilland Mosquito and Bristol Beaufighter were in used in operations overseas, the squadron having many detachments during this period.

The Bristol Brigand was flown while at Tengah, Singapore in 1952 against terrorists in Malaya, and later the Hornet F Mk 3 in the same role. The first Jet fighter used by No 45 Squadron was the Vampire and then the Meteor, but only for a short time in 1955. The squadron was flying the Venom FB Mk 1 in Hong Kong when it was disbanded.

Reformed in 1957 at Coningsby on Canberra B Mk 2s, markings were now to be seen as the Squadron's Winged Camel emblem was applied to the Canberra's tail. The Canberra remained in operation until February of 1970 when the unit again disbanded.

Reformed at RAF West Raynham on Hunter FGA Mk 9s in 1972 the squadron moved to RAF Wittering a month later, its role being that of ground attack, providing a reserve of trained strike pilots. The Hunters now bore more colorful markings applied to the nose section comprising a Blue rectangle with Red diamonds and the Squadron emblem on a White circular field. The Hunters of No 45 Squadron carried individual aircraft numbers, and at one point they also carried code letters in White on the aircraft tail, which were repeated in black on the nosewheel doors. The unit disbanded at RAF Wittering in 1976.

Hawker Hunters known to be on strength with No 45 Squadron
FGA Mk 9 - XG130 (A), XK137 (42), XG130 (61), XG261 (64), XE582 (70),
T Mk 7 - XL619 (77)

NO 54 SQUADRON

Formed on 15 May 1916, No 54 Squadron began operations with the Sopwith Pup and the Sopwith Camel when it was posted to France during World War I.

The Squadron disbanded in the UK after the war but was to reform again in 1930, equipped with the Siskin for a while, then the Bristol Bulldog, Gloster Gauntlet and finally the Gloster Gladiator, before being re-equipped with the Spitfire in March of 1939.

The Squadron flew various marks of the Spitfire throughout World War II until converting to the Hawker Tempest in 1945. The first Jet to be operated was the Vampire F Mk1 in 1946, and was replaced by the F Mk 3 version in 1948. With these aircraft the Squadron made a notable first in aviation history when the squadron flew its fighters across the Atlantic on a goodwill tour of Canada and the US. The Vampires were replaced with Meteor F Mk 8s in 1953. These camouflaged aircraft carried rectangles each side of the fuselage roundel containing twelve Blue and Yellow checkers.

On 14 February 1955, the first Hunter F Mk 1 (WT696) arrived at Odiham. Shortly after the Hunters arrived the Squadron formed a four ship Aerobatic Team. New Blue and Yellow checkers were positioned on the nose, flanking a Blue Rampant Lion. Dark Blue wing tips and nosewheel doors were also carried, as well as aircraft letters in Yellow. There were also special markings in the form of colored tails; the Squadron Commander's aircraft, WT692 (S), had a Gold tail with a Blue lightning streak, and the Officer Commanding (OC) A Flight had a Red tail with a Yellow flash, while the aircraft belonging to the OC of B Flight, WW636 (Q), was Blue with a Yellow flash.

The F Mk 1 remained with the unit until September of 1955 when it was superseded by the F Mk 4. The nose markings remained the same but the nosewheel doors were now Silver with the aircraft letter in Black. In 1957 the Hunter F Mk 6 entered service with the unit with the markings changing only slightly. The Lion emblem was placed on a white circular field and the checkers were reduced from twelve to eight on each side of the Lion.

In 1960 when the unit converted to the Hunter FGA Mk 9 the markings were the same as on the F Mk 6 variant, but when posted to RAF West Raynham in 1963, a blue code letter on a Yellow circular field was added to the tail, and one aircraft had a Blue nose wheel door containing a Yellow letter. The Squadron CO had a Blue Lion and his flag on Silver.

By 1966 all Hunters of No 54 Squadron carried Blue nosewheel doors with a row of Yellow checkers and a Yellow aircraft letter, which was repeated in Yellow on the tail. The wing tips were painted white. The Hunter soldiered on with No 54 until 1969, when it was reformed at RAF Coningsby on the Phantom FGR Mk 2.

Hawker Hunters known to have been on strength with No 54 Squadron
F Mk 1 - WT692 (S), WT696 (O), WT659 (U), WT681 (R), WT558 (T), WW610 (A)
WW641 (B), WW636 (Q)
F Mk 4 - XF998 (A), XE661 (B), WT708 (F), WT764 (G), WV281 (M)
F Mk 6 - XG273 (L), XF509 (M), XF421 (P), XE645 (P)
FGA Mk 9 - XG260 (B), XG207 (C), XG264 (D), XE552 (M), XG155 (T), XF517 (V)

(Above) Hunter F Mk 1s of No 54 Squadron's Aerobatic team. The Commander of 'B' Flight's aircraft, with a lightning bolt on the tail, is in the lead. 1955 (RAF Museum)

(Above) Hunter F Mk 5, WP186 (AW), of 56 Squadron assigned to the Officer Commanding (OC) of the RAF Waterbeach Flying Wing in January of 1958. The OC's aircraft carries checkered wingtips of both squadrons of the wing, Red and White above (No 56 Squadron), and Black and Yellow below (No 63 Squadron). The OC's initials are painted in White on the tail above the fin flash. (Map)

NO 56 SQUADRON

Formed at Gosport on 8 June 1916, No 56 Squadron received the S.E.5A Fighter. Later equipment included the Snipe, Grebe and Bulldog between 1924 and 1936.

The Hurricane came on strength with the Squadron in 1938, all colors were dropped and the Squadron codes were the only means of identification, this continued with the Hawker Typhoon, Spitfire and Tempest in 1944.

With the arrival of the Meteor F Mk 4 at RAF Thorney Island during 1948, code letters flanking the roundel remained the standard. However, by 1950 the fuselage checkers had returned, initially on the Meteor F Mk 4s before being replaced by the Meteor F Mk 8s. The Unit was based at RAF Waterbeach early in 1954 when the Meteor started being replaced by the Swift F Mk 1 and F Mk 2. No 56 Squadron was the first Squadron to receive the type, but so many teething troubles existed with the Swift that it was replaced by the Hunter F Mk 5 in May of 1955.

The Hunters carried Red and White checkers on the sides of the nose and on the wing tips. In the center of the nose markings was a Blue circular field on which a White aircraft letter was superimposed. A small White sloping letter was at the base of the tail. On the nose wheel door was a large Red letter, although some early aircraft carried Black nosewheel letters. By 1957 the aircraft letter on the Blue background was being replaced by the Phoenix Squadron emblem.

The Squadron commander flew WP104 (A), with three Red and White checkers on the nosewheel door bordered by a Light Blue stripe, both above and below. Hunter WP186 (AW), flown by Wing Commander A.R. Wright, OC of the Flying Wing at Waterbeach, lacked the nose markings but carried wing tip Red and White checkers on the upper surfaces, and Yellow and Black checkers on the lower surfaces. The lower surface checkers was for No 63 Squadron which was the other Waterbeach resident. The Station title 'Waterbeach' was painted in Black diagonally across the nose wheel door.

In 1958 the unit replaced its F Mk 5s with the F Mk 6 version, and moved from Waterbeach to RAF Wattisham, Suffolk. The Hunter F Mk 6 retained the Squadron markings but carried a White letter with a Red outline on the nosewheel doors. The Hunter began to be replaced in 1961 by the Lightning F1A.

Hawker Hunters known to be on strength with No 56 Squadron
F Mk 5 - WP104 (A), WP186 (AW), WN992 (D), WN979 (E), WN986 (H),
WN970 (M), WP125 (R)
F Mk 6 - XF516 (E), XE648 (H), XG229 (M), XE594 (N), XG159 (P).

(Below) Hunter F Mk 5, WP104 (A), assigned to the Commander of No 56 Squadron. Red and Yellow checkers are carried on both the nose and wingtips. The nose checkers are on both sides of the squadron emblem, a Phoenix on a Blue circle.

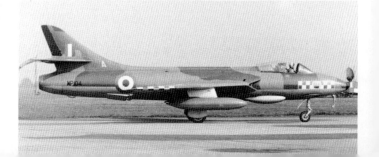

Hunter F Mk 5, WP186, carrying the camouflage pattern applied to all Hunter variants.

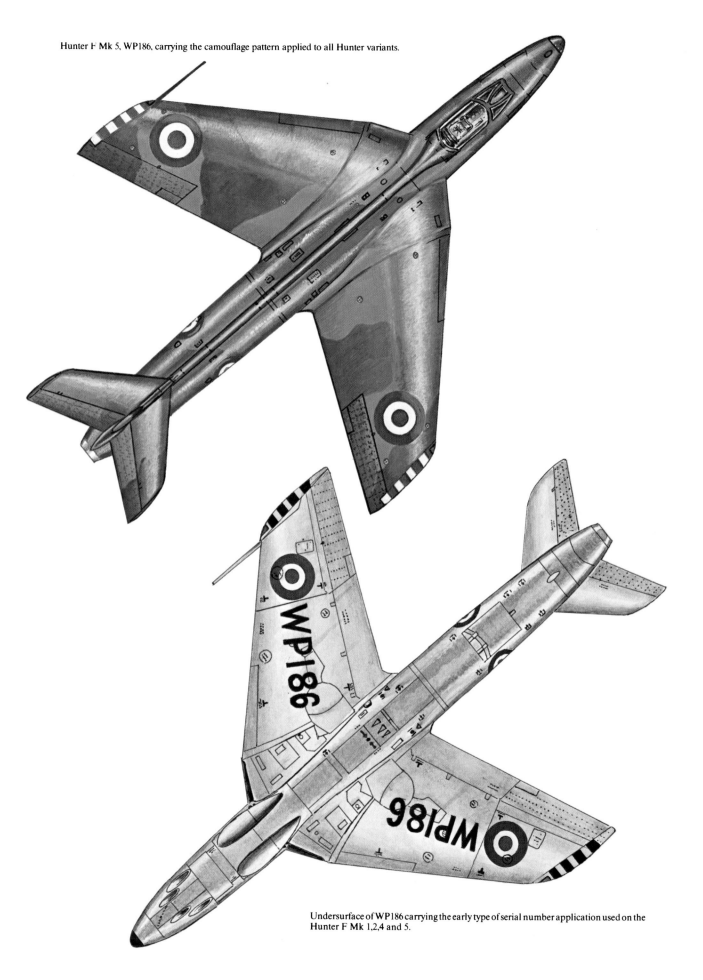

Undersurface of WP186 carrying the early type of serial number application used on the Hunter F Mk 1,2,4 and 5.

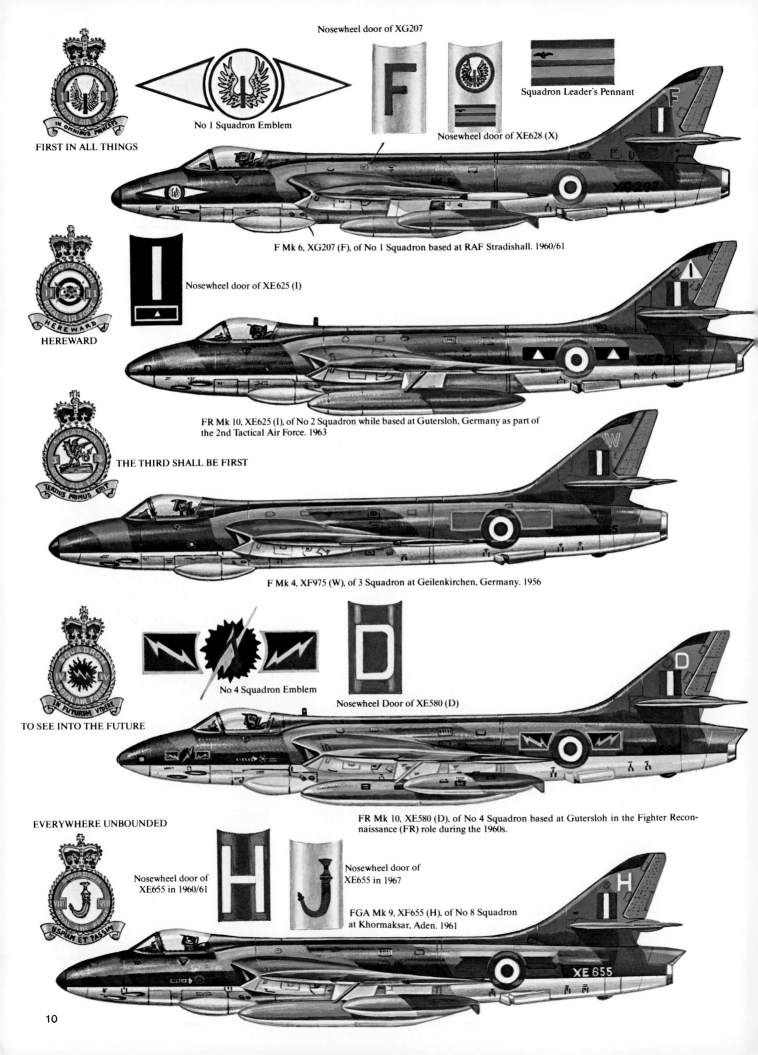

Nosewheel door of XG207

No 1 Squadron Emblem

Squadron Leader's Pennant

Nosewheel door of XE628 (X)

FIRST IN ALL THINGS

F Mk 6, XG207 (F), of No 1 Squadron based at RAF Stradishall. 1960/61

Nosewheel door of XE625 (I)

HEREWARD

FR Mk 10, XE625 (I), of No 2 Squadron while based at Gutersloh, Germany as part of the 2nd Tactical Air Force. 1963

THE THIRD SHALL BE FIRST

F Mk 4, XF975 (W), of 3 Squadron at Geilenkirchen, Germany. 1956

No 4 Squadron Emblem

Nosewheel Door of XE580 (D)

TO SEE INTO THE FUTURE

EVERYWHERE UNBOUNDED

FR Mk 10, XE580 (D), of No 4 Squadron based at Gutersloh in the Fighter Reconnaissance (FR) role during the 1960s.

Nosewheel door of XE655 in 1960/61

Nosewheel door of XE655 in 1967

FGA Mk 9, XF655 (H), of No 8 Squadron at Khormaksar, Aden. 1961

FGA Mk 9, XE645 (SW), carrying both No 8 and No 43 Squadron markings. 1968

RAF Khormaksar Station Crest

Flight 1417 colors with station crest

Nosewheel door of XE599

FR Mk 10, XE599 (DW) of 1417 Flight. Although still part of No 8 Squadron, 1417 Flight removed the fuselage markings of No 8 Squadron once the Flight had been formed.

No 14 Squadron Emblem

I SPREAD MY WINGS AND KEEP MY PROMISE

Nosewheel door of XJ646 (D)

F Mk 6, XJ646 (D) at Wetherfield's AFD display in 1962.

THEY CAN BECAUSE THEY THINK THEY CAN

Nosewheel door of XG191 (G)

F Mk 6, XG191 (G), based at Leconfield in 1963

Later nosewheel door of XF457 (V)

No 20 Squadron Emblem

Nosewheel door of XF457 (V)

FGA Mk 9, XF457 (V), of No 20 Squadron at Tengah, Singapore during the 1960s.

DEEDS NOT WORDS

11

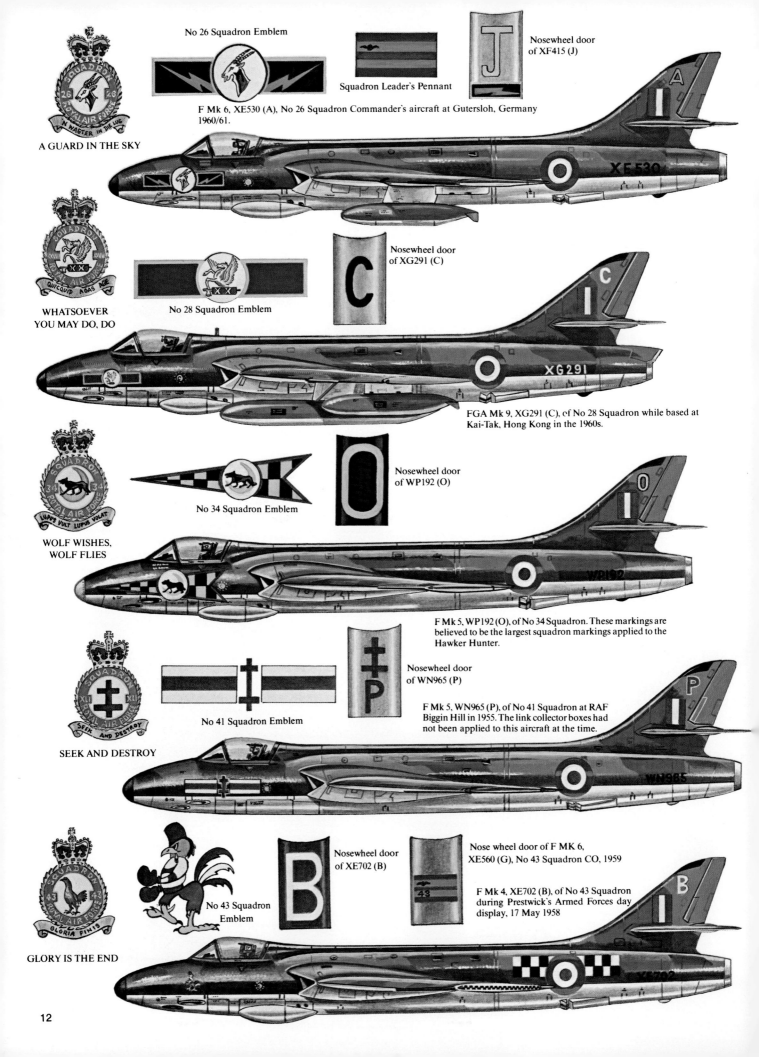

No 26 Squadron Emblem

Squadron Leader's Pennant

Nosewheel door of XF415 (J)

A GUARD IN THE SKY

F Mk 6, XE530 (A), No 26 Squadron Commander's aircraft at Gutersloh, Germany 1960/61.

WHATSOEVER YOU MAY DO, DO

No 28 Squadron Emblem

Nosewheel door of XG291 (C)

FGA Mk 9, XG291 (C), of No 28 Squadron while based at Kai-Tak, Hong Kong in the 1960s.

WOLF WISHES, WOLF FLIES

No 34 Squadron Emblem

Nosewheel door of WP192 (O)

F Mk 5, WP192 (O), of No 34 Squadron. These markings are believed to be the largest squadron markings applied to the Hawker Hunter.

SEEK AND DESTROY

No 41 Squadron Emblem

Nosewheel door of WN965 (P)

F Mk 5, WN965 (P), of No 41 Squadron at RAF Biggin Hill in 1955. The link collector boxes had not been applied to this aircraft at the time.

GLORY IS THE END

No 43 Squadron Emblem

Nosewheel door of XE702 (B)

Nose wheel door of F MK 6, XE560 (G), No 43 Squadron CO, 1959

F Mk 4, XE702 (B), of No 43 Squadron during Prestwick's Armed Forces day display, 17 May 1958

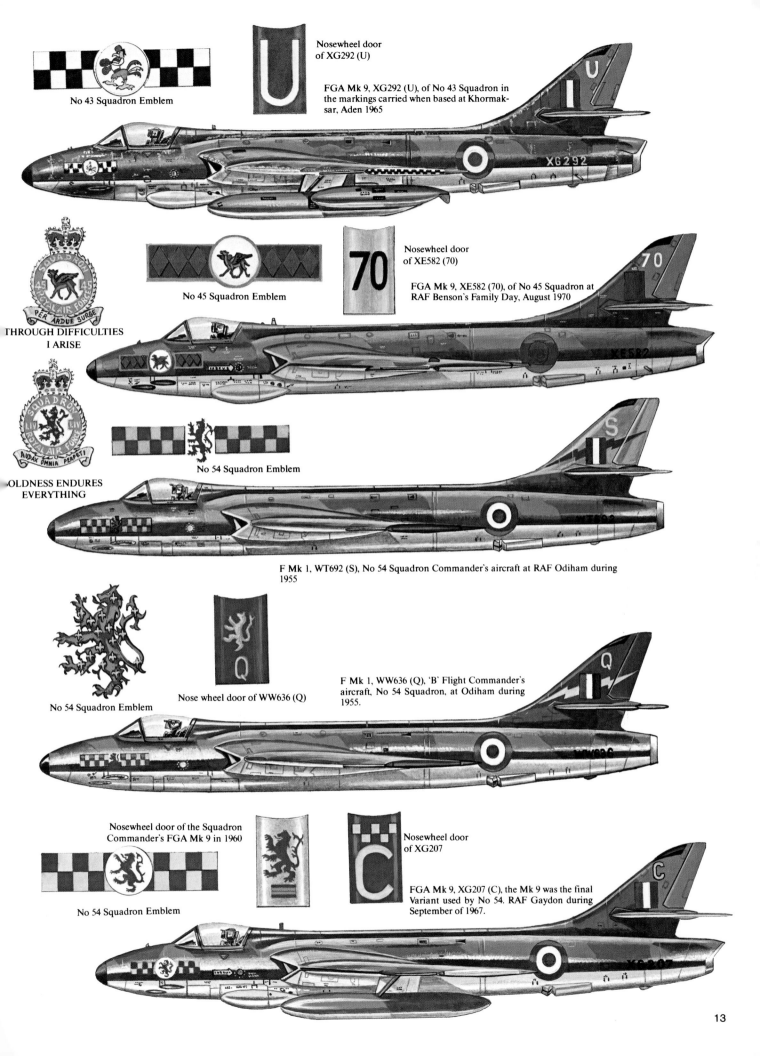

No 43 Squadron Emblem

Nosewheel door of XG292 (U)

FGA Mk 9, XG292 (U), of No 43 Squadron in the markings carried when based at Khormaksar, Aden 1965

No 45 Squadron Emblem

THROUGH DIFFICULTIES I ARISE

Nosewheel door of XE582 (70)

FGA Mk 9, XE582 (70), of No 45 Squadron at RAF Benson's Family Day, August 1970

No 54 Squadron Emblem

BOLDNESS ENDURES EVERYTHING

F Mk 1, WT692 (S), No 54 Squadron Commander's aircraft at RAF Odiham during 1955

No 54 Squadron Emblem

Nose wheel door of WW636 (Q)

F Mk 1, WW636 (Q), 'B' Flight Commander's aircraft, No 54 Squadron, at Odiham during 1955.

Nosewheel door of the Squadron Commander's FGA Mk 9 in 1960

No 54 Squadron Emblem

Nosewheel door of XG207

FGA Mk 9, XG207 (C), the Mk 9 was the final Variant used by No 54. RAF Gaydon during September of 1967.

13

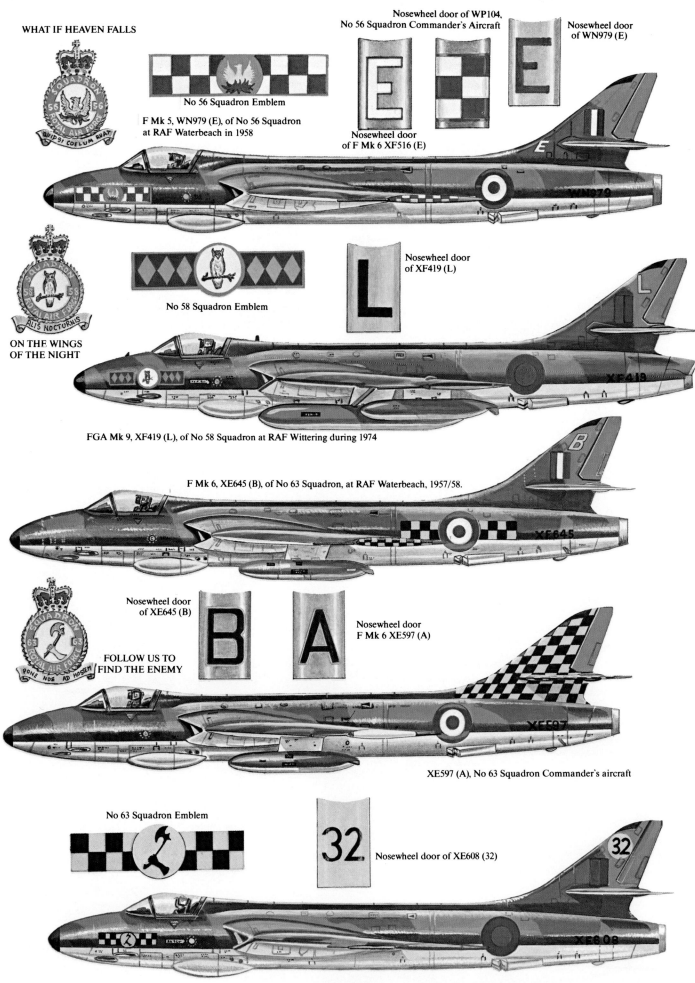

WHAT IF HEAVEN FALLS

No 56 Squadron Emblem

F Mk 5, WN979 (E), of No 56 Squadron
at RAF Waterbeach in 1958

Nosewheel door of WP104,
No 56 Squadron Commander's Aircraft

Nosewheel door
of WN979 (E)

Nosewheel door
of F Mk 6 XF516 (E)

No 58 Squadron Emblem

ON THE WINGS
OF THE NIGHT

Nosewheel door
of XF419 (L)

FGA Mk 9, XF419 (L), of No 58 Squadron at RAF Wittering during 1974

F Mk 6, XE645 (B), of No 63 Squadron, at RAF Waterbeach, 1957/58.

Nosewheel door
of XE645 (B)

FOLLOW US TO
FIND THE ENEMY

Nosewheel door
F Mk 6 XE597 (A)

XE597 (A), No 63 Squadron Commander's aircraft

No 63 Squadron Emblem

Nosewheel door of XE608 (32)

F Mk 6, XE608 (32), of No 63 Squadron after reforming at RAF Chivenor, No 229 OCU.
Although carrying 'B' type roundels and fin flashes, this aircraft retained the high gloss
finish. 1972/73

Hunter F Mk 6, carrying 'B' type roundels and Grey undersurfaces. The camouflage has been extended to wrap around the leading edge onto the undersurfaces of the wings.

Undersurface of Hunter F Mk 6, XE597 (63 Squadron Commander's aircraft), carrying the later serial number application.

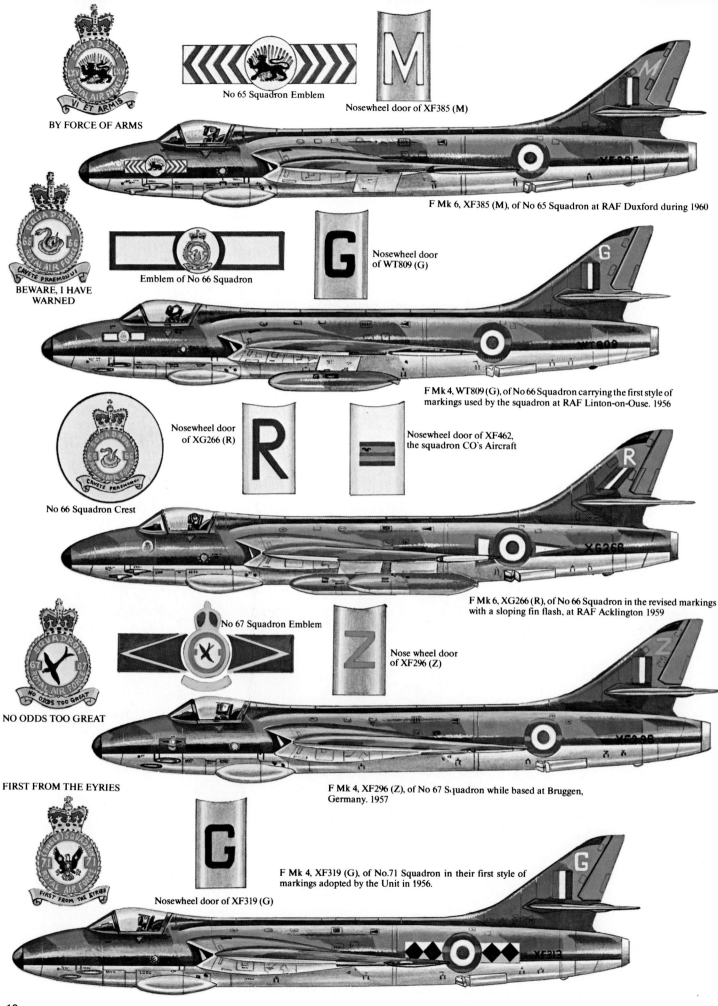

BY FORCE OF ARMS

No 65 Squadron Emblem

Nosewheel door of XF385 (M)

F Mk 6, XF385 (M), of No 65 Squadron at RAF Duxford during 1960

BEWARE, I HAVE WARNED

Emblem of No 66 Squadron

Nosewheel door of WT809 (G)

F Mk 4, WT809 (G), of No 66 Squadron carrying the first style of markings used by the squadron at RAF Linton-on-Ouse. 1956

Nosewheel door of XG266 (R)

Nosewheel door of XF462, the squadron CO's Aircraft

No 66 Squadron Crest

F Mk 6, XG266 (R), of No 66 Squadron in the revised markings with a sloping fin flash, at RAF Acklington 1959

No 67 Squadron Emblem

Nose wheel door of XF296 (Z)

NO ODDS TOO GREAT

FIRST FROM THE EYRIES

F Mk 4, XF296 (Z), of No 67 Squadron while based at Bruggen, Germany. 1957

F Mk 4, XF319 (G), of No.71 Squadron in their first style of markings adopted by the Unit in 1956.

Nosewheel door of XF319 (G)

FIRST FROM THE EYRIES

No 71 Squadron Emblem

F Mk 4, XF938 (D), in the final markings of No 71 Squadron. 1957

No 74 Squadron Emblem

I FEAR NO MAN

Nosewheel door of WV 334 (E)

F Mk 4, WV334 (E), of No 74 Tiger Squadron with White tail markings adopted for exercise Vigilant which was held between 25 and 27 May 1957.

No 79 Squadron Emblem

NOTHING CAN STOP US

229 OCU Crest

BY LEARNING YOU WILL LEAD

Nosewheel door of XE626 (9)

FR Mk 10, XE626 (9), of No 79 Squadron, 229 OCU at RAF Chivenor during 1970.

No 92 Squadron Hunter F Mk 4 nose markings 1956/57

No 92 Squadron Hunter F Mk 6 Nose markings 1957 to mid 1959

EITHER FIGHT OR DIE

F Mk 6, XG186 (J), of No 92 Squadron with revised Squadron markings and raked fin flash. Tail checkers were adopted after 1957.

Nosewheel door of XG186 (J)

XG186 (J) of the Blue Diamonds Aerobatic team. This was the first aircraft of the Squadron to be painted in the Royal Blue team colors. 1961

No 92 Squadron F Mk 6 nose markings from mid 1959 to 1962

Nosewheel door of XG186 (J) after Blue paint

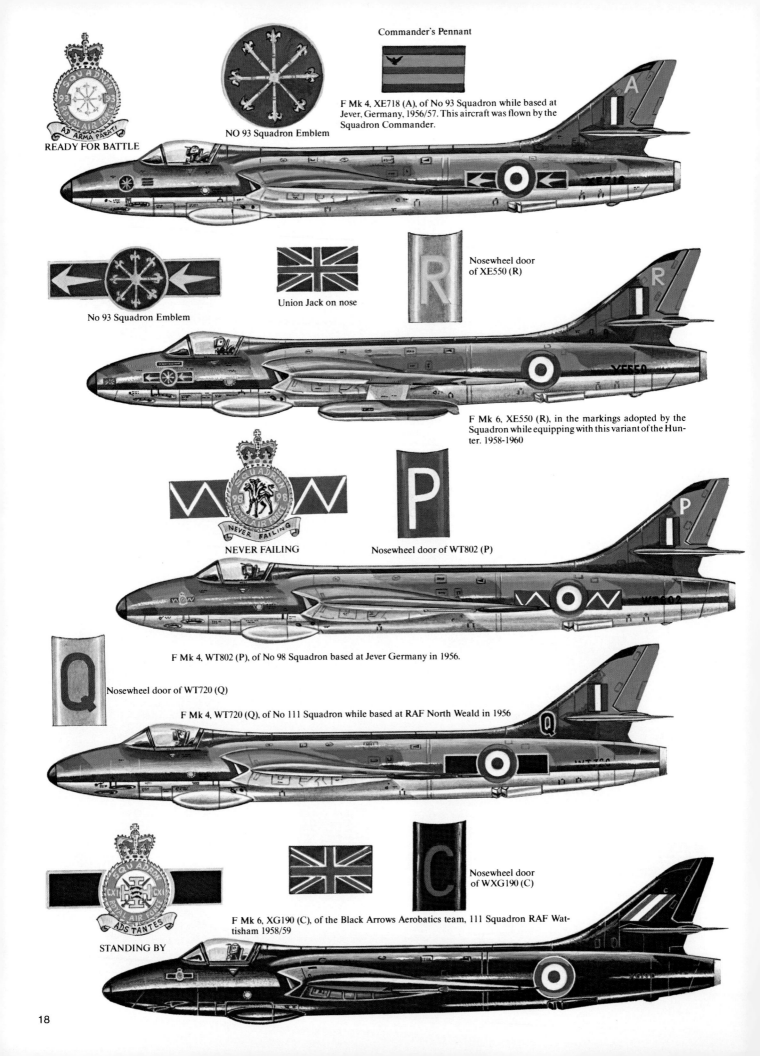

READY FOR BATTLE

NO 93 Squadron Emblem

Commander's Pennant

F Mk 4, XE718 (A), of No 93 Squadron while based at Jever, Germany, 1956/57. This aircraft was flown by the Squadron Commander.

No 93 Squadron Emblem

Union Jack on nose

Nosewheel door of XE550 (R)

F Mk 6, XE550 (R), in the markings adopted by the Squadron while equipping with this variant of the Hunter. 1958-1960

NEVER FAILING

Nosewheel door of WT802 (P)

F Mk 4, WT802 (P), of No 98 Squadron based at Jever Germany in 1956.

Nosewheel door of WT720 (Q)

F Mk 4, WT720 (Q), of No 111 Squadron while based at RAF North Weald in 1956

STANDING BY

Nosewheel door of WXG190 (C)

F Mk 6, XG190 (C), of the Black Arrows Aerobatics team, 111 Squadron RAF Wattisham 1958/59

18

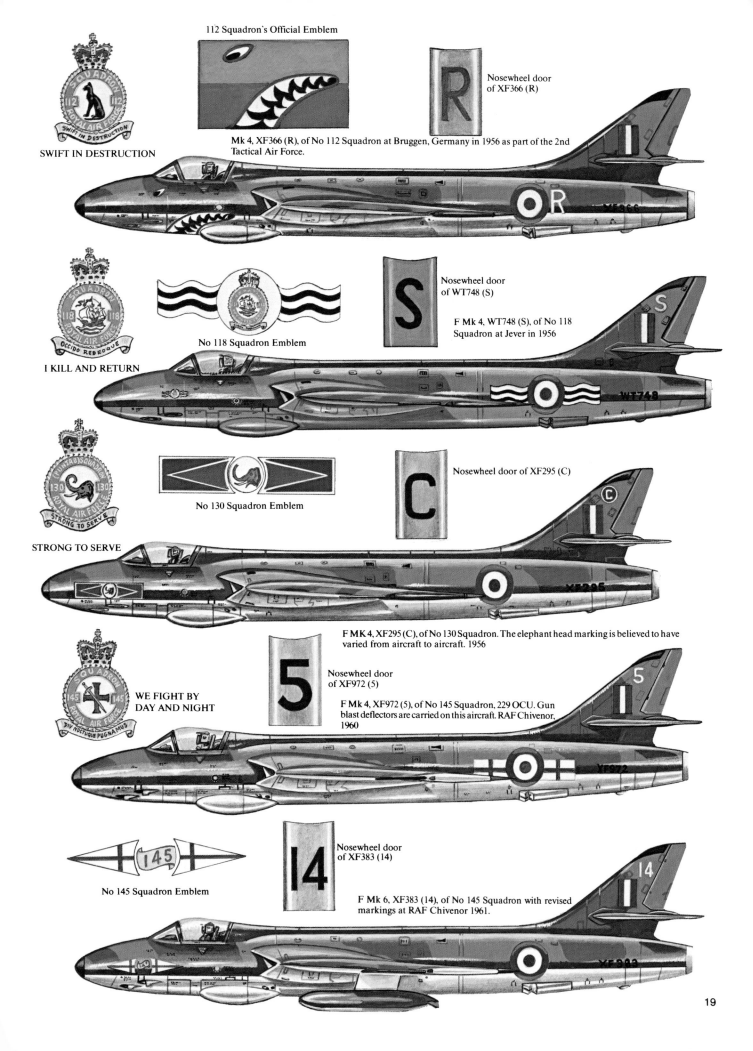

112 Squadron's Official Emblem

SWIFT IN DESTRUCTION

Nosewheel door of XF366 (R)

Mk 4, XF366 (R), of No 112 Squadron at Bruggen, Germany in 1956 as part of the 2nd Tactical Air Force.

I KILL AND RETURN

No 118 Squadron Emblem

Nosewheel door of WT748 (S)

F Mk 4, WT748 (S), of No 118 Squadron at Jever in 1956

STRONG TO SERVE

No 130 Squadron Emblem

Nosewheel door of XF295 (C)

F MK 4, XF295 (C), of No 130 Squadron. The elephant head marking is believed to have varied from aircraft to aircraft. 1956

WE FIGHT BY DAY AND NIGHT

Nosewheel door of XF972 (5)

F Mk 4, XF972 (5), of No 145 Squadron, 229 OCU. Gun blast deflectors are carried on this aircraft. RAF Chivenor, 1960

No 145 Squadron Emblem

Nosewheel door of XF383 (14)

F Mk 6, XF383 (14), of No 145 Squadron with revised markings at RAF Chivenor 1961.

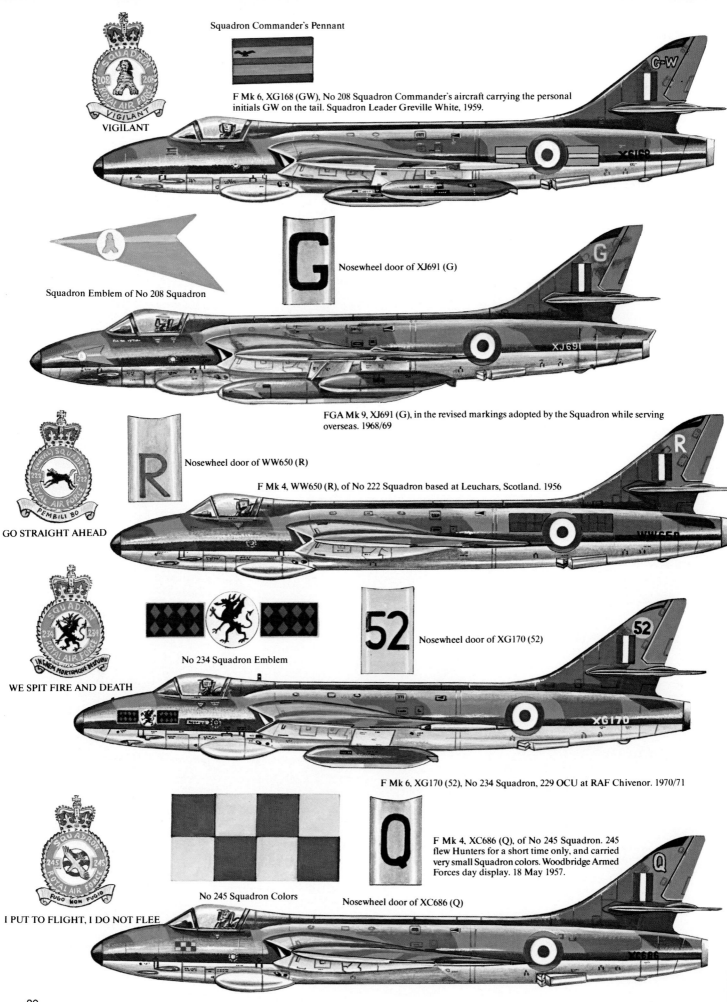

Squadron Commander's Pennant

F Mk 6, XG168 (GW), No 208 Squadron Commander's aircraft carrying the personal initials GW on the tail. Squadron Leader Greville White, 1959.

VIGILANT

Squadron Emblem of No 208 Squadron

Nosewheel door of XJ691 (G)

FGA Mk 9, XJ691 (G), in the revised markings adopted by the Squadron while serving overseas. 1968/69

GO STRAIGHT AHEAD

Nosewheel door of WW650 (R)

F Mk 4, WW650 (R), of No 222 Squadron based at Leuchars, Scotland. 1956

WE SPIT FIRE AND DEATH

No 234 Squadron Emblem

Nosewheel door of XG170 (52)

F Mk 6, XG170 (52), No 234 Squadron, 229 OCU at RAF Chivenor. 1970/71

I PUT TO FLIGHT, I DO NOT FLEE

No 245 Squadron Colors

Nosewheel door of XC686 (Q)

F Mk 4, XC686 (Q), of No 245 Squadron. 245 flew Hunters for a short time only, and carried very small Squadron colors. Woodbridge Armed Forces day display. 18 May 1957.

20

Control Column

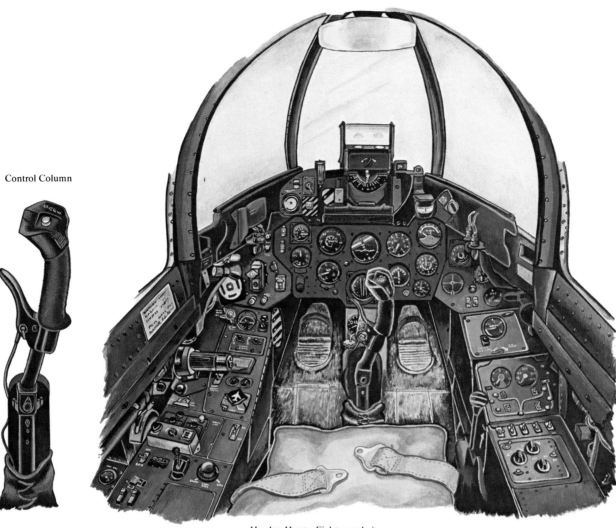

Hawker Hunter Fighter cockpit.

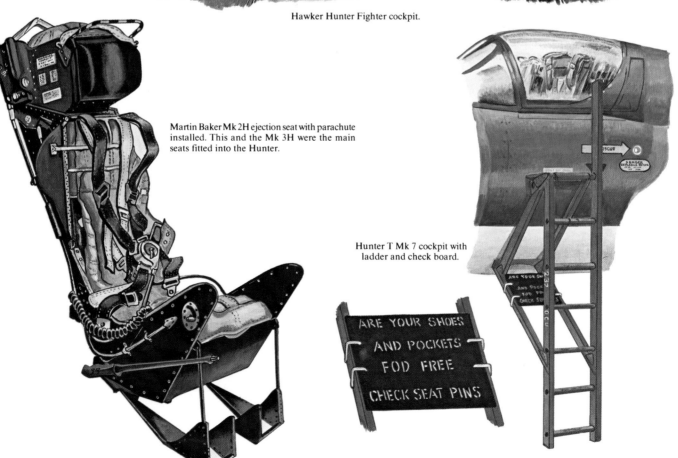

Martin Baker Mk 2H ejection seat with parachute installed. This and the Mk 3H were the main seats fitted into the Hunter.

Hunter T Mk 7 cockpit with ladder and check board.

ARE YOUR SHOES
AND POCKETS
FOD FREE
CHECK SEAT PINS

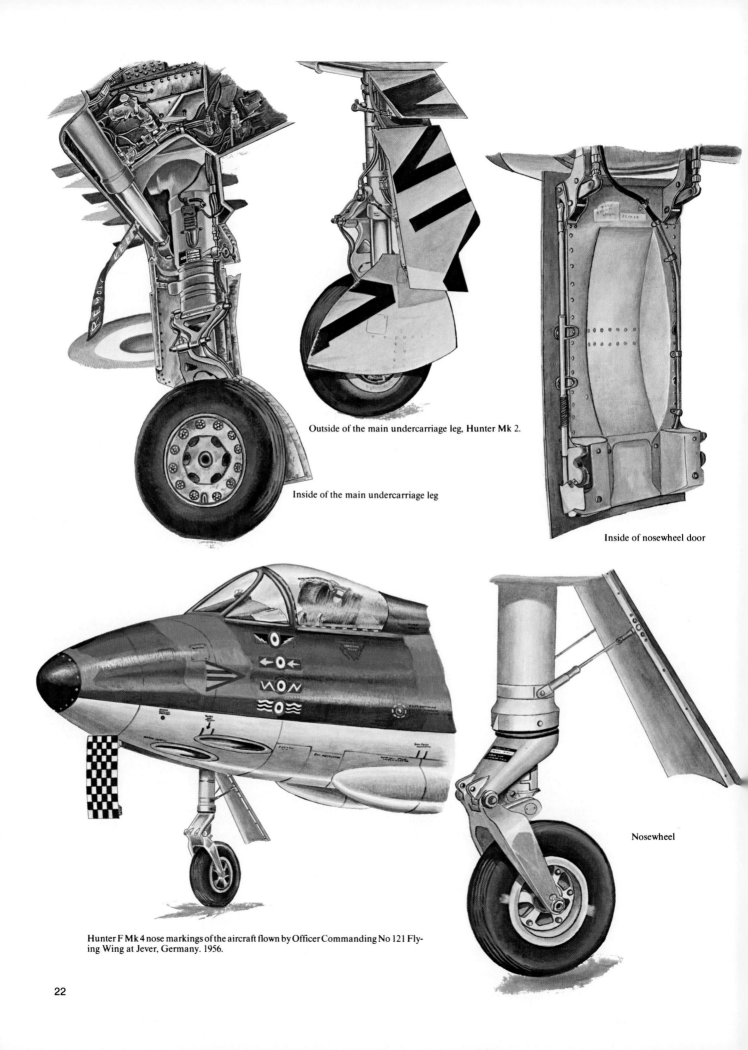

Outside of the main undercarriage leg, Hunter Mk 2.

Inside of the main undercarriage leg

Inside of nosewheel door

Nosewheel

Hunter F Mk 4 nose markings of the aircraft flown by Officer Commanding No 121 Flying Wing at Jever, Germany. 1956.

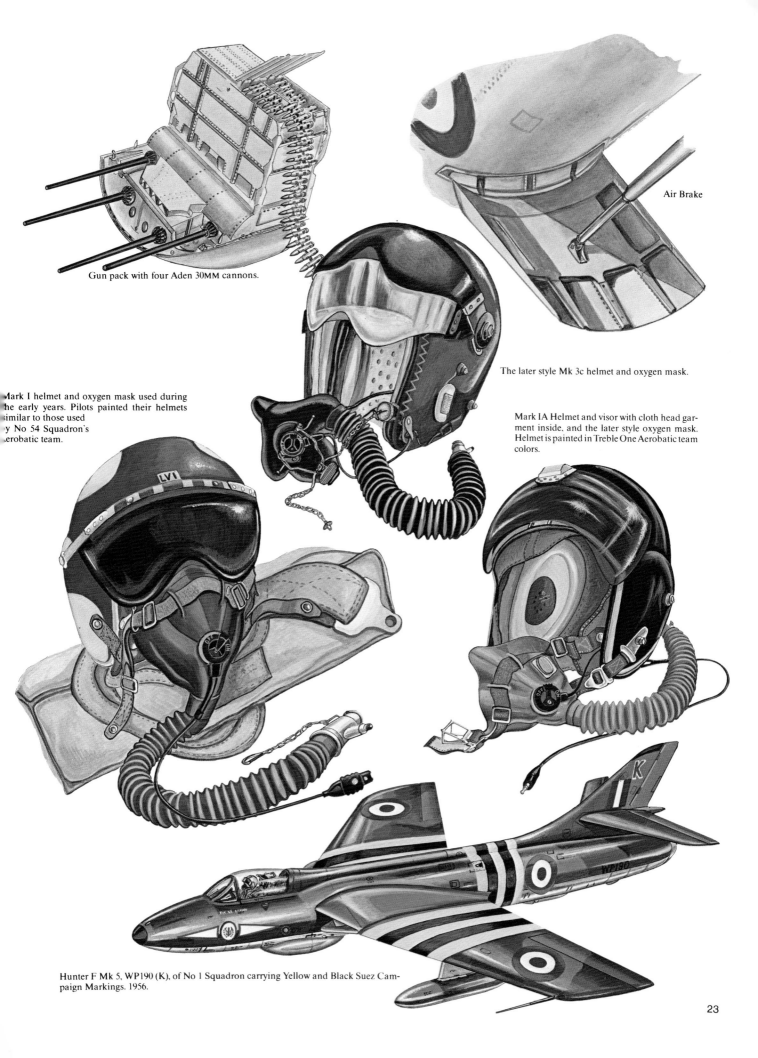

Gun pack with four Aden 30MM cannons.

Air Brake

The later style Mk 3c helmet and oxygen mask.

Mark I helmet and oxygen mask used during the early years. Pilots painted their helmets similar to those used by No 54 Squadron's Aerobatic team.

Mark IA Helmet and visor with cloth head garment inside, and the later style oxygen mask. Helmet is painted in Treble One Aerobatic team colors.

Hunter F Mk 5, WP190 (K), of No 1 Squadron carrying Yellow and Black Suez Campaign Markings. 1956.

RISE FROM THE EAST

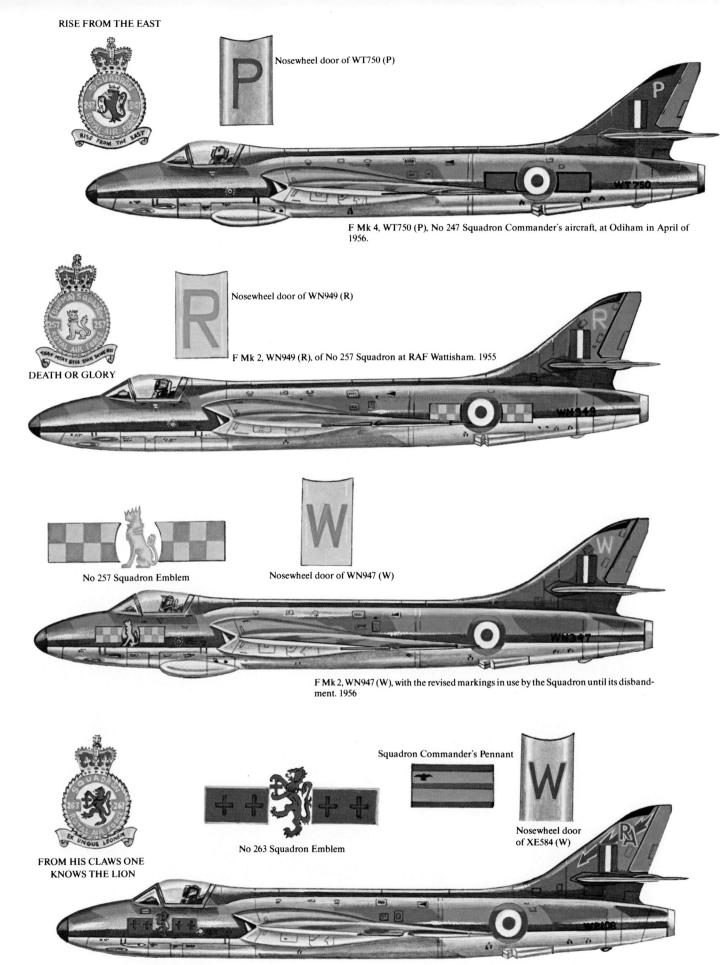

Nosewheel door of WT750 (P)

F Mk 4, WT750 (P), No 247 Squadron Commander's aircraft, at Odiham in April of 1956.

Nosewheel door of WN949 (R)

F Mk 2, WN949 (R), of No 257 Squadron at RAF Wattisham. 1955

DEATH OR GLORY

No 257 Squadron Emblem

Nosewheel door of WN947 (W)

F Mk 2, WN947 (W), with the revised markings in use by the Squadron until its disbandment. 1956

FROM HIS CLAWS ONE
KNOWS THE LION

No 263 Squadron Emblem

Squadron Commander's Pennant

Nosewheel door
of XE584 (W)

F Mk 5, WP108 (RA), No 263 Squadron Commander's aircraft. Squadron Leader R Aytoun, RAF Wattisham, 1956.

(Above) FGA Mk 9, XJ686 (41) of No 58 Squadron carrying a 230 gallon drop tank under each wing. Squadron motif is a Blue rectangle with Green diamonds flanking a White circle containing the squadron's owl emblem.

NO 58 SQUADRON

Originally a Bomber Squadron, No 58 was formed in Northumberland on 10 January 1916. In 1917 it was operating on the Western Front flying F.E.2Bs where it was to remain for a year before converted to the Handley Page H.P.0/400.

In 1924 the Squadron began flying the Vickers Virginia. After flying the Anson and Whitley, in 1942 the squadron was assigned to Coastal Command flying the Halifax as a reconnaissance unit, and later flew Mosquitos with Coastal Command.

During 1950 the Squadron was transferred to Bomber Command carrying out Photo Reconnaissance duties flying Canberras PR Mk 3s, Mk 7s and Mk 9s. It was based at RAF Wyton from 1953 to 1970 while operating these variants of the Canberra, disbanding there in 1970.

The squadron reformed at RAF Wittering on 1 August 1973 with Hunter FGA Mk 9s, undertaking the strike role which it shared with No 45 Squadron. The Hunters of No 58 Squadron carried Markings on the sides of the nose that were similar in design to the markings of No 45 except that the colors were Green diamonds on a Blue backing, with the Squadron Owl emblem on a White circle in the center. The individual aircraft letter or number was in Yellow on the tail and repeated in Black on the nosewheel door. The Squadron remained at RAF Wittering until disbanding in 1976.

Hawker Hunters known to have been on strength with No 58 Squadron
FGA Mk 9 - XF442 (81), XK140 (P), XK140 (92), XJ656 (41), XJ694 (94), XG291 (83)

(Above) F Mk 6, XE597 (A), in immaculate condition, and carrying Black and Yellow checkers on the tail belongs to the Commander of No 63 Squadron. 1958 (Map).

NO 63 SQUADRON

No 63 Squadron was formed on 5 July 1916 at Stirling, Scotland. Originally slated to go to France the squadron was diverted to Mesopotamia where it flew R.E.8s against Turkey.

Disbanded in 1920 the squadron was re-formed as a bomber unit in February of 1937 receiving the Fairey Battle in May. During WW II it operated the Mustang 1 and the Spitfire V in the reconnaissance role, between 1942 and 1945.

It was assigned the Spitfire LF Mk 16 in 1946 which it operated until 1948. The last squadron in Fighter Command to fly the Spitfire, which was replaced in June of 1948 by the Gloster Meteor F Mk 4. The Black and Yellow checkered markings were first applied to the fuselage sides of the Meteor F Mk 4 and were continued on the Meteor F Mk 8s in 1950.

During 1956 the Hawker Hunter F Mk 6 began to replace the Meteor. The checker markings were perpetuated on sides of the the Hunters, flanking the fuselage roundel, and on the wingtips. A Yellow aircraft letter sloping rearward was applied to the tail, and repeated on the nosewheel door in Black with a Yellow border.

The Squadron Commander's aircraft, XE597 (A), lacked the fuselage markings but carried a checkerboard covering the complete vertical and horizontal tail surfaces, while the wing tips were painted White. The aircraft letter 'A' was applied to the nose wheel door. The squadron markings remained this way until the squadron disbanded at RAF Waterbeach in October of 1958.

Hawker Hunters known to be on strength with No 63 Squadron
F Mk 6 - XE597 (A), XG271 (F), XG130 (J), XE561 (R), XG187 (V)

(Below) F Mk 6, XE647 (E), of No 63 Squadron with Black and Yellow Checkers on the fuselage and wingtips while based at RAF Waterbeech in 1958.

NO 63 Squadron of the 229 OPERATIONAL CONVERSION UNIT

Upon reforming on 1 January No 63 Squadron became a training squadron, or Shadow Squadron serving within the 229 Operational Conversion Unit (OCU). No 63 Squadron's responsibility was to turn out nine trained Day Fighter Ground Attack (DFGA) pilots and seven pre-Lightning pilots every four months. The Squadron's task also included training Pilot Attack Instructors (PAI's), and conduct Forward Air Control (FAC) courses. The Squadron also held an operational role in the event of war, and to achieve this aim it was equipped with Hunter F MK 6s, FGA Mk 9s, and T Mk 7s.

The Squadron's Black and Yellow checkerboard markings were applied to the sides of the aircraft's nose with the Squadron emblem in the center. White individual aircraft letters were carried on the tails, and repeated in Black on the nosewheel door. For a while the aircraft of No 63 had their spines painted White for identification purposes. The practice was not carried on for long and the unit reverted to the normal markings.

By 1969 Yellow discs with Black numbers were seen on the tails along with Yellow nosewheel doors with Black numbers. In 1971 the B type roundel was introduced into service again. Lacking the white area, these roundels were applied to the wings, fuselage, and to the tail in the form of a Flash. The markings remained the same although White tail letters were to re-appear, especially on the Hunter FGA Mk 9. The Hunter served with No 63 Squadron until May of 1979 when they began to be replaced by the Hawk T Mk 1.

Hawker Hunters known to have been on strength with No 63 Squadron (OCU)
F Mk 6 - XF526 (38), XE608 (32), XF439 (3)
FGA Mk 9 - XJ634 (29), XG254 (K)

(Above) F Mk 6, XF507 (A), of No 65 Squadron without drop tanks looks very clean at RAF Shepherd's Grove during an Armed Forces Day display on 17 May 1958. The squadron rectangle is White with Red chevrons on either side of the squadron emblem, a lion in a White circle.

NO 65 SQUADRON

This Squadron began life as a Training Unit when it was formed at Wyton in August of 1916. Its main equipment was the Sopwith Camel with which it flew in 1917 as a Fighter unit, moving to France later that year. The Squadron returned to the UK in 1919 and was disbanded.

Reforming in 1934 as a Night Fighter Squadron it operated the Hawker Demon. It was based at RAF Hornchurch in 1936 and equipped with the Gloster Grebe and later the Gladiator.

The unit entered the Second World War equipped with the Spitfire Mk 1 which it had received during the spring of 1939. The squadron went on to operate other variants of the Spitfire, the Mk IIa in 1941, the Mk VB and the Mk IX in 1944. The Mustang Mk III and Mk IV were next, followed by the Spitfire Mk 16 in 1945 and the D.H. Hornet in 1947.

During April of 1951 the Meteor F Mk 8 came on strength with the squadron which was now based at RAF Duxford, Cambridgeshire. The Meteors carried Red chevrons on each side of the fuselage roundel until March of 1957 they were replaced by the Hunter F Mk 6. Squadron markings were now applied to the sides of the nose and comprised of Red chevrons on White rectangles with a Lion emblem in the center of a White background. White wing tips were to be seen later on, while a Yellow sloping aircraft letter was painted on the tail and repeated in White with a Red outline on the nose wheel door. 65 Squadron operated the Hunter until March of 1961 when the unit disbanded at Duxford.

Hawker Hunters known to be on strength with 65 Squadron
F Mk 6 - XF507 (A), XG433 (G), XF447 (H), XF385 (M), XE593 (P)
T Mk 7 - XL600

(Above) This Hunter F Mk 6, XF462, was assigned to the Commander of No 66 Squadron. The coiled rattlesnake emblem on a White circle replaced the aircraft letter above the fin flash. Squadron Leader's pennant was carried on the nosewheel door. RAF Acklington in September of 1958. (Map)

(Above) T Mk 7, XL620, of No 66 Squadron in overall Silver with a Yellow training band around the fuselage. The Squadron emblem is on a Blue disc. RAF Acklington 1960.

NO 66 SQUADRON

Like No 65 Squadron this unit served as a training squadron when it was formed in June of 1916. It re-equipped with the Sopwith Pup and moved to France in 1917, flying Patrols and Bomber escorts.

In 1936 the Gloster Gauntlet came on to Squadron strength and served until October 1938 when it was replaced by the Spitfire Mk I while the squadron was at Duxford. The unit operated the Spitfire Mk II in 1942 alongside the Mk Vb variant. The Spitfire Mk VI and LF Mk 9 were next operated and finally the LF Mk 16 version in 1944. The Spitfire was replaced by the Gloster Meteor F Mk 3 in 1947.

No 65 Squadron moved to RAF Linton-on-Ouse in 1949, flying the Meteor F Mk 4, which were still carrying Squadron code letters on the fuselage sides. However, with the introduction of the Meteor F Mk 8 variant in 1951 squadron colors were once again introduced, being made up of White rectangles with Blue borders. These markings were transferred to the Sabre F Mk 4 which was flown by the Squadron from 1953 to 1956. The squadron was one of only two within Fighter Command to fly the Sabre F Mk 4, the other squadrons flying the Sabre being with the 2nd Tactical Air Force in Germany.

The Sabre had been an interim Fighter and in March of 1956 it began being replaced by the Hunter F Mk 4. The rectangular markings carried on the fuselage sides of the Sabres were carried on the sides of the nose of the Hunters, with the Squadron crest on a White disc in the center. White aircraft letters were carried on the tail, and repeated in Black on Silver nosewheel doors. The Squadron Commander's aircraft bore a Blue tail and his initials 'A F O' in Yellow, and a White lightning streak.

No 65 Squadron moved to RAF Acklington in early 1957, converting to the Hunter F Mk 6, after having flown the F Mk 4 for only a year. The F Mk 6 retained the nose style markings until July of 1958, when a pennant design was adopted and applied to the fuselage sides. White wing tips were carried and the Squadron crest was retained on the nose. The White aircraft letters were retained on the tail but the nosewheel doors were now painted White with Blue aircraft letters.

A Hunter, serialed XF462, became the Commander's aircraft carrying a Rattle Snake emblem on a White circle on the tail above the fin flash in the place of the code letter. During 1959 the Squadron began carrying swept back fin flashes. The Hunter served with No 66 Squadron until disbanding at RAF Acklington on 30 September 1960.

Hawker Hunters known to have been on strength with No. 66 Squadron
F Mk 4 - WT809 (G), WV385 (L), XE681 (J), WV409 (N)
F Mk 6 - XG253 (A), XG237 (C), XE618 (E), XF517 (G), XG153 (L), XG266 (R), XE544 (V), XF462
T Mk 7 - XL620

(Above) F Mk 4 of No 67 Squadron, not only were the markings rather small, but they were seldom carried. (RAF Museum)

NO 67 SQUADRON

No 67 Squadron was formed on 16 March 1916 from No 1 Australian Flying Corps during its sailing from Australia to the Middle East and the Suez Canal. Its first equipment was the Bristol F.2.B. which took part in operations against the Turkish Armies during 1918. The unit saw all of its service overseas during World War I and II and flew aircraft such as the Brewster Buffalo in 1941, the Hawker Hurricane in 1942 to 1944, and the Spitfire Mk VIII from February of 1944 to 1945.

The Squadron was disbanded while overseas in July of 1945, and was re-formed at RAF Wattisham during the autumn of 1950, and eventually took the Vampire F.B. Mk 5 as its mount. When it moved to Wildenrath in Germany as part of the 2nd Tactical Air Force it replaced the Vampire with Sabre F Mk 1s in 1953. The Sabres carried Red and Blue rectangular markings on the fuselage sides on each side of the roundel.

After finally settling at Bruggen early in 1956 where the Sabre was replaced by the Hunter F Mk 4. The Hunter would see service from 1956 to 1957, when the unit was disbanded at Bruggen.

Very little has been seen of No 67 Hunters and it would appear that only two or three aircraft actually bore Squadron colors. No 67 Squadron markings comprised a small Squadron crest applied to the nose section flanked by Red rectangles with Blue centers. Light Blue aircraft letters were applied to the tails and nose wheel door.

Hawker Hunters known to have been on strength with No 67 Squadron
F Mk 4 - WV273 (D), XE717 (G), XE689 (W), XF296 (Z)

NO 71 SQUADRON

Formed in March 1917, No. 71 Squadron first flew Sopwith Camels. Shortly after the war, the Squadron disbanded and did not reform until September of 1940, when it flew the Hurricane. The Squadron was based at RAF Church Fenton, and was made up with a lot of American volunteer pilots, hence the Bald Eagle and title on the squadron emblem. The unit went on to fly the Spitfire Mk II and Mk Vb, ending its RAF service at Debden, when No 71 Squadron was transferred to the USAAF becoming the 334 Squadron of the 4th Pursuit Group.

In 1950 No 71 Squadron was reformed at Gutersloh flying the Vampire FB Mk 5, which was replaced by the Sabre F Mk 1 and F Mk 4 in 1953. The Sabres carried the Eagle emblem in a White disc on the aircraft's nose, later White and Yellow rectangles containing Black diamonds flanked the fuselage roundels.

In May of 1956 the Hunter F Mk 4 began to arrive and for a while markings similar to those carried on the Sabres were perpetuated, however, these were moved to the sides of the Hunter's nose with the Eagle in the center. Aircraft letters were painted in White on the tails and Black on the nosewheel doors. The unit flew the Hunter F Mk 4 until 1957 when it was disbanded at Bruggen.

Hawker Hunters known to have been on strength with No 71 Squadron
F Mk 4 - XF938 (D), XF313 (G), XF367.

(Above) F Mk 6, XF511 (P), belonging to No 74 'Tiger' Squadron at Wethersfield's Armed Forces Day display on 28 May 1960. The squadron Tiger emblem was flanked by rectangles made of Yellow and Black triangles that resembled tiger stripes.

NO 74 SQUADRON

Formed in July of 1917, No 74 Squadron was originally a training Squadron, however, after receiving the S.E.5a in 1918 it became a Fighter Squadron. Disbanding in 1919, it was reformed in Malta during 1935 on Hawker Demons and then the Gloster Gauntlet, which it kept until 1939.

Squadron markings were carried on aircraft as early as the Gauntlet but were discontinued when the squadron began flying Spitfires and Hurricanes. The Squadron's first jet aircraft were Meteor F Mk 3s in 1945. The Meteor F Mk 4 and F Mk 8 was flown between 1948 and 1957, during which time the aircraft were Silver overall. However, by 1951 the Meteor F Mk 8 began carrying Black and Yellow tiger markings instead of the codes. By 1954 these aircraft were being camouflaged but retained the squadron colors.

During 1957, No 74 Squadron was based at RAF Horsh St Faith, Norfolk when it began to receive the Hunter F Mk 4. Markings were painted on the Hunter's nose with the Tiger head in the center. Yellow aircraft letters were carried on the tail, and repeated in Black on the nosewheel door. In June of 1957 some aircraft had their tails and wing tips painted White for exercise 'Vigilant', one of the United Kingdom's defense exercise. The Squadron moved to RAF Coltishall in 1969 and the Hunters were replaced by the Lightning F.1.

Hawker Hunters known to have been on strength with No 74 Squadron
F Mk 4 - WT720 (B), XF940 (F), XE683 (G), WV269 (H), WV371 (N)
F Mk 6 - XF504 (B), XK141 (F), XE610 (J), XK142 (L), XE511 (P), XG198 (Q)

NO 79 SQUADRON

No 79 Squadron was formed on 8 August 1917 and was initially engaged in the Training role but early in 1918 it became a fighter squadron flying the Sopwith Dolphin.

Disbanded in France during 1919, it reformed in 1937 at RAF Biggin Hill on the Gloster Gauntlet. The Gauntlet was operated for about a year when replaced by the Hawker Hurricane, which the squadron would fly until converting to the Thunderbolt Mk II in 1944, carrying out mainly ground attack and bombing missions. In December of 1945 the unit disbanded again.

Reformed in 1951 in the Fighter Reconnaissance (FR) role, No 79 Squadron was assigned to Buckenburg in Germany under the 2nd Tactical Air Force. Flying the Meteor FR Mk 9 and later the Swift FR Mk 5 it disbanded again in 1961. No 79 Squadron was reformed at RAF Chivenor Devon, as a shadow Squadron within No 229 OCU. A reserve unit in the Fighter Reconnaissance role it operated a small number of Hunter FR 10s, F Mk 6s and later the FGA Mk 9 variant. Pilots were trained in the specialized reconnaissance and fighter attack role.

Squadron markings of White rectangles with Red arrows flanked the fuselage roundel, however, tail markings varied over the years with White aircraft code letters on the tails and Black ones on the nose wheel doors being applied at one stage. In 1970 No 79 aircraft were seen with White tail numbers, and still later Black numbers on a Yellow disc were carried. However, in 1975 Hunter FAA Mk 9s were carrying White letters, and later numbers again.

In 1974 the unit moved to Brawdy, assigned to No 1 Tactical Weapons Unit, the emblem of which was carried on the nose of the Hunters.

Hawker Hunters known to be on strength with No 79 Squadron
F Mk 6 - XJ637 (10), XG130 (30), XF439 (26)
FGA Mk 9 - XG207 (C), XF376 (D), XG194 (A)
FR Mk 10 - XG168 (10), WW594 (11), XE626 (9)

(Above) F Mk 4, XF324 (D), of No 92 Squadron carrying the early style markings that were replaced after a year by two maple leafs and a cobra emblem. September 1956.

(Below) F Mk 6, XG229 (F), of 92 Squadron, the only squadron to carry checkers under the tail planes. The checkers totalled eighteen pairs. RAF Middleton St George in 1957.(Map)

After a years service with the Squadron, the F Mk 4 was replaced by the Hunter F Mk 6. Markings carried on the F Mk 6 were similar to those found on the earlier F Mk 4 variant except that the Squadron emblem and Yellow disc were replaced by two maple leaves and a Cobra emblem on the camouflaged background. A row of checkers was added to the area below the tail planes and by 1960 a raked fin flash and White wing tips had been added. The emblem on the nose was changed to a single maple leaf and cobra on a White disc, still flanked by the Red and Yellow checkers.

Blue Diamonds

In 1961, the Squadron became the RAF's official Aerobatic Team, taking over from the famous Black Arrows, III Squadron Aerobatic Team. Aerobatic Team aircraft were painted in Royal Blue overall with White markings on the fuselage and wing tips. The nose checkers and emblem were retained and a minute White code letter was applied to the tail just above the fin flash, which was repeated on the nosewheel door in a slightly larger format. Later these code letters were changed to Black on the tail, but remained White on the wheel door. The Blue Diamonds had up to sixteen Hunters on its rolls during its service.

The Hunters terminated service at RAF Leconsfield in 1963 when the Lightning Fighter replaced it in the Squadron.

Hawker Hunters known to have been on strength with No 92 Squadron
F Mk 4 - WT719 (B), WV314 (B), XF324 (D), XE705 (F), WV389 (G)
XE659 (J), WV323 (K), XE706 (L), XF973 (M)
F Mk 6 - XG211 (H), XF552 (D), XE532 (L), XF321 (H), XF520 (K), XF516 (N),
XG198 (Q),
T Mk 7 - XL605 (T)
BLUE DIAMONDS - XE532 (L), XE656 (B),XF520 (K), XF521 (X), XF552 (D)
XG137 (E), XG159 (W), XG185 (Z), XG186 (J), XG189 (M)
XG190 (N), XG194 (P), XG201 (R), XG211 (A), XG225 (S)
XG228 (C), XG231 (H), XG232 (G)
T Mk 7 - XL571 (V)

NO 92 SQUADRON

No 92 Squadron was formed on 1 September 1917 at London Colney, and flew the S.E.5a in battles over the Somme in 1918. A year later the unit disbanded and was not reformed until 1939 at RAF Tangmere where it flew Blenheims as a bomber squadron before again becoming a fighter squadron flying Spitfire Mk Is. No 92 Squadron moved to RAF Biggin Hill in 1941, flying the Spitfire Mk V until 1943 when it was replaced by the Mk IX. During World War II the Squadron became the RAF's highest scoring unit with some 317 enemy aircraft to its credit.

In 1949 No 92 Squadron was based at RAF Linton-on-Ouse Yorkshire, flying the Meteor F Mk 4, followed by the F Mk 8 in 1950. When flying the Sabre F Mk 4 in 1954, the unit was the second one in Fighter Command to use this aircraft. During the spring of 1956 Hunter F Mk 4s began to arrive, and the markings were repositioned to the Hunter's nose with the Squadron crest in the center on a Yellow circular field. Yellow aircraft letters with Black outlines were carried on the tails, and repeated in Black on the nosewheel door.

NO 93 SQUADRON

No 93 Squadron was formed on 7 December 1940 as a bomber squadron equipped with the Handley Page Harrow. The Harrow served for only a few months when the Wellington joined it, serving for the same length of time. These aircraft were used for experimenting with towing mines into the path of oncoming aircraft. The Douglas Havoc joined the squadron, being used in the same role. However, in 1942 Spitfire Mk Vs replaced the bombers and the squadron took on the fighter role. The Spitfire Mk V was flown until 1943, when the Mk IX was taken on strength. The Mustang Mk 4 was flown next, but only for a few months before the Squadron was disbanded in December of 1946.

It was reformed again in 1950 at Celle, Germany under the 2nd Tactical Air Force and operated the Vampire FB Mk 5 for four years before receiving the Sabre F Mk 1 in 1954. The Sabres began carrying Blue rectangular markings with Yellow arrows positioned on each side of the fuselage roundels.

Hunter F Mk 4s replaced the Sabre in 1956 and carried essentially similar markings.

(Above) T Mk 7 trainer, XL571 (V), in overall Royal Blue was assigned to the Blue Diamonds in 1961. (Map)

(Below) F Mk 6, XG180 (N), painted overall Royal Blue belongs to the Blue Diamonds Aerobatic team of No 92 Squadron, carrying the later style emblem. XG186 (J) was the first aircraft painted by the Squadron.

The aircraft letters were Yellow, and were carried on both the tail and nosewheel door.The Squadron emblem, a Yellow Escarbuncle was painted on the sides of the nose in a Blue disc. The unit was based at Jever in Germany when the Hunter F Mk 6 joined the Squadron in 1958. Markings were now changed with the rectangles being re-positioned to the nose, flanking a somewhat smaller squadron emblem. Wing tips were painted Yellow, and the aircraft letters remained Yellow. No. 93 Squadron operated the Hawker Hunter until 1960 when the unit disbanded at Jever in December.

Hawker Hunters known to have been on strength with No. 93 Squadron
F Mk4 - XE718 (A), XE685 (B)
XE677 (Q), WV267 (R)
WV364 (S) F Mk6 - XJ635 (F),
XE550 (R) XJ634 (V) XJ717 (Z)

NO 111 SQUADRON

Treble One Squadron was formed on 1 August 1917 in Palestine and was equipped with a variety of aircraft. In 1920, the Squadron was re-numbered, becoming No 14 Squadron. Reformed at RAF Duxford in 1923 with Sopwith Snipes and Gloster Grebes, No 111 Squadron became part of the fighter defense of the UK. Black Squadron markings were being applied to the aircraft and continued onto the Gauntlets in 1936.

With the outbreak of World War II, Treble One had the honor of being the first unit to receive the Hurricane, and later flew the Spitfire Mk I, Mk II, Mk V and Mk IX, ending in 1947 when the unit was disbanded.

In 1953 the unit reformed at RAF North Weald flying the Meteor F Mk 8. Black rectangular markings with Yellow outlines were carried on the fuselage sides of these camouflaged Fighters.

The Hunter F Mk 4 replaced the Meteor in 1955, with markings flanking the roundel. A Black aircraft letter with Yellow outlines were applied to the base of the tail and repeated in Red on Silver nosewheel doors.

No 111 formed an Aerobatic Team in 1956 of five aircraft. Serials numbers were WV321 (E), WT716 (D), WV327 (U), WV379 (V) and XE679 (B), all were in standard camouflage.

In November of 1956, the Squadron received the Hunter F Mk 6 and was chosen as the RAF's official Aerobatic Team, representing Fighter Command in 1957. The team was led by Squadron Leader Roger Topp who had previously led the Hunter F Mk 4 team. Aircraft of the aerobatic team were painted in High Gloss Black overall with a Raked Fin Flash and small Red fuselage serial numbers, and the aircraft letter was in Red on the nosewheel door. Later a Union Jack was applied to the starboard side of the nose and a small Red aircraft letter was applied to the tail above the fin flash.

During 1958, The Black Arrows as they were known, moved to RAF Wattisham under the command of Squadron Leader Peter Latham. Black Arrow aircraft now had White outlines added on the roundels and fin flashes, and Yellow outlined rectangles flanking the Squadron crest on the portside of the nose. The number of aircraft was increased from five to nine, and eventually as many as twenty-two, with all twenty-two aircraft actually completing a loop at the SBAC Display.

1960 was the last year for the team, No 111 Squadron re-equipped with the Lightning F Mk 1A in 1961. Treble One's Hunters were distributed to other units, some going to 92 Squadron, and some going to No 229 OCU such as XG200 which retained its Black overall scheme for quite sometime in 1962, carrying a White 5 above the fin flash.

Hawker Hunters known to be on strength with No 111 Squadron
F Mk 4 - WT759 (B), XE679 (B), WT710 (N), WT720 (Q), WV379 (V)
F Mk 6 - XG193 (A), XG201 (B), XG190 (C), XG189 (D), XG171 (E), XG129 (F)
XF506 (F), XG170 (G), XG203 (H), XJ715 (H), XG194 (N), XE592 (P) XG200 (Q),
XF446 (R), XE653 (S), XF419 (T), XG160 (U), XF430 (V) XF525 (X) T Mk 7 XL610

(Below) Five No 111 Squadron Hunter F Mk 6s in the all Black Scheme adopted when they became Fighter Command's official Aerobatic Team. (RAF Mod.)

(Below) The Black Arrows in a line abreast formation. White outlines to the roundels have been added. (RAF Mod.)

(Above) Mk 4, WW656 (N), of No 98 Squadron about to go into a loop. The fuselage rectangles were Red containing a jagged White stripe. (RAF Museum)

NO 98 SQUADRON

No 98 Squadron was a Bomber Squadron when it was formed on 30 August 1917, and equipped with the De Havilland 9 when it was sent to France during World War I. The Squadron saw service until the summer of 1919 when it was disbanded.

It was reformed again in the Bomber role, during February of 1936 and equipped with the Hawker Hind. The Hind was operated until 1938 when it was replaced by the Fairey Battle, which was used in Iceland as part of Coastal Command during 1942. The Squadron later equipped with the North American Mitchell Mk II, taking part in bombing raids over Belgium. After the war the Mosquito was flown, but the squadron's role changed to fighter attack when the Vampire FB Mk 5 was taken on strength. Later the Venom FB 1 was flown.

The Squadron moved to Jever in 1955, becoming the first Squadron in Germany to fly the Hunter. No 98 Squadron's Hunter F Mk 4s carried Red and White rectangles flanking the fuselage roundels and repeated on the sides of the nose in a much smaller format with the Squadron badge in the center. Aircraft letters were in White on the tails, and repeated in White on Red nosewheel doors.

Hunters were flown by No 98 Squadron until December of 1956 when the Squadron was disbanded at Jever.

Hawker Hunters known to have been on strength with No 98 Squadron
F Mk 4 - WT742 (A), WW655 (M), WW656 (N), WW658 (O), WT802(P)
XE667 (Z), WN647 (C), WN649 (E

(Above) Shark's teeth markings decorated the noses No 112 Squadron's Hunters. (Map)

NO 112 SQUADRON

After forming on 30 July 1917 No 112 Squadron's first aircraft was the Sopwith Pup. The squadron did not see action in France during World War I and was disbanded in 1919. Reformed in 1939 it flew the Gloster Gladiator until 1941, after which the squadron flew Curtis Tomahawks carrying shark mouth markings from 1941 until 1944, when the Mustang Mk III and Mustang Mk IV replaced them. Shark mouth markings were carried on these aircraft also.

After the war No 112 Squadron disbanded, but was reformed at Fassberg, Germany in 1951 as part of the 2nd TAF operating Vampire FB Mk 5s, again carrying shark mouth markings. While based at Bruggen in 1954, the Sabre F Mk 1 and F Mk 4 replaced the Vampires and were similarly marked.

With the introduction of the Hunter F Mk 4 in April of 1956, the shark's teeth and eye markings were perpetuated. Aircraft letters were White and applied to the fuselage sides aft of the roundel and repeated in Red on the nosewheel doors. One Hunter (XF319), bearing a question mark (?) instead of an aircraft letter, may well have been the Squadron Commander's Fighter.

Hunters were the last aircraft to serve with No 112 Squadron, it disbanded at Bruggen in May of 1957.

Hawker Hunters known to have been on strength with No 112 Squadron
F Mk 4 - WV412 (A), XE674 (D), XF307 (F), XF293 (N), XF366(R), XF937 (T) XF319 (?)

(Above) This immaculate Hawker Hunter was flown by the Squadron Commander of 118 Squadron. The graceful Black and White wavy lines of No 118 Squadron flank the fuselage roundel. (RAF Mod)

NO 118 SQUADRON

The Squadron was originally formed in January 1918 but after serving as a training unit for some ten months it was disbanded.

Reformed as a Fighter Squadron in 1941, flying the Spitfire throughout most of the war, receiving the Mustang Mk III in 1945.

After the war the squadron was disbanded, but was reformed as a 2nd TAF fighter squadron in 1951 at Fassberg, operating the Vampire and Venom Fighter Bomber.

The Hunter F Mk 4s, which replaced the Venoms in 1956, carried somewhat unusual markings applied to the Hunter's fuselage sides consisting of Black and White wavy lines, which were repeated on the sides of the nose in a smaller format, flanking the Squadron crest. The aircraft letters were Yellow on the tails and Black on the nosewheel doors. One Hunter, serialed WT748 (S), had its lower surfaces painted in the earlier cerulean (PR Blue) scheme previously applied to 2nd TAF Sabres. The number of Hunters painted in this scheme is unknown.

The Hunter F Mk 6 is reputed to have served with No 118 Squadron, but to date there is no evidence of this. It is possible that Mk 6s were on loan to the squadron before its disbanding in 1962.

Hawker Hunters known to have been on strength with No 118 Squadron
F Mk 4 - XE665 (A), WT768 (C), WW637 (G), WT737 (N), XE710 (R) XF368 (N), WT748 (S), WT753 (E), XE703 (B)

(Below) F Mk 4, WT748, of No 118 Squadron at RAF Bruggen. This aircraft is unusual in having Photo Reconnaissance Blue on the under surfaces, which is beginning to peel off the link collector box and main undercarriage door. (RAF Museum).

(Above) A 130 Squadron Hunter undergoing maintenance at Bruggen, Germany. No 130 began carrying an elephant head in a White disc when the squadron motif was moved to the nose when the Hunter F Mk 4 was introduced in May of 1956. (RAF Museum)

NO 130 SQUADRON

No 130 Squadron was formed at Portreath in Cornwall on 20 June 1941. Flying Spitfire Mk IIs, it carried out shipping patrols around Cornwall's coastline, later flying various marks of the Spitfire including the Mk V, Mk XIV and IX.

Moving to RAF Odiham in July of 1946, it was re-equipped with Vampire F Mk 1s, and less than a year later was re-numbered to No 72 Squadron.

It was reformed again as No 130 Squadron at Bruggen, Germany in April 1953, flying the Vampire FB Mk 5 until February of 1954, when it re-equipped with Sabre F Mk 1 and F Mk 4s. The Sabres began carrying Blue rectangles with Red diamonds outlined in White, painted on each side of the fuselage roundel.

With the introduction of the Hunter F Mk 4 in May of 1956, the markings were moved to the side of the nose with the Indian Elephants head emblem centered on a white disc. Aircraft letters were White on a Blue disc, just above the fin flash and repeated in Black on the nosewheel door.

Hunters were the last aircraft operated by the Squadron before it disbanded at Bruggen in 1957.

Hawker Hunters known to have been on strength with No 130 Squadron
F Mk 4 - XF292 (A), XF294 (B), XF295 (C), XF298 (E), XF308 (F), XF321 (G)

(Above) F Mk 6, XF383 (14), of 145 Squadron of the 229 OCU at Alconbury's Armed Forces Day display on 17 June 1961. The Yellow scroll carried the numerals 145 and was flanked by White pennants with Red crosses. (Map)

NO 145 SQUADRON

Formed in 1918, No 145 was operational with S.E.5s during the latter part of World War I and was disbanded in October of 1919.

When reforming in 1939, it was based at Croydon flying the Bristol Blenheim in the Day and Night Fighter role, but by early 1940 it had re-equipped with the Hawker Hurricane. In 1942, the Squadron moved overseas to the Western Desert where it operated the tropicalised Spitfire Mk Vc, Spitfire Mk IX, and later the Mk VIII, moving to Malta, Sicily, Italy, and eventually disbanding at Treviso in August 1945.

During early 1952, No 145 reformed at Celle, Germany flying Vampire FB Mk 5s in the Fighter Bomber role but replaced these aircraft with the Venom FB Mk 1 in 1954. This aircraft was operated until October 1957 when the unit once again disbanded.

The Squadron reformed again at RAF Civenor, Devon in November of 1957, as a reserve squadron, used in the Training role within No 229 OCU. The aircraft operated was the Hunter F Mk 4 and T Mk 7. Squadron markings were applied to the fuselage sides from September of 1959 consisting of White rectangles, each with a Red cross super-imposed, with White wing tips being applied later. A White aircraft number was applied to the sides of the tail and repeated in Black on the nosewheel door.

During 1961 the Hunter F Mk 6 began to replace the Mk 4 variant, with the markings being moved to the nose. Now consisting of White pennants, they retained the Red crosses and added a Yellow scroll containing the squadron number in Red in the center of the design. The Hunter F Mk 6 also had White wing tips and retained the aircraft numbers in White and Black as on the F Mk 4. During 1963 the squadron transferred to No 226 OCU at RAF Middleton St George, which was the Lightning Training Unit. The Hunters remained at Chivenor and were absorbed into other units.

Hawker Hunters known to have been on strength with No 145 Squadron
F Mk 4 - XF991 (4), XF972 (5)
F Mk 6 - XF387 (4), XG226 (6), XE644 (7), XF385 (11), XF383 (14)
XJ715 (15), XJ715 (15),
XL587 (91)

(Above) FGA Mk 9, XJ632 (B), of No 208 Squadron based at Khormaksar in the Middle East during 1967.

(Above) 234 Squadron markings on a Hunter F Mk 4 while based in Germany. The White circular backing to the Griffon emblem was not applied until the Squadron reformed within the 229 OCU. (Map)

NO 208 SQUADRON

Formed in October of 1916 No 208 Squadron flew offensive patrols on the Western Front, returning to the United Kingdom in 1919 it disbanded.

Reformed in 1920 from 113 Squadron and sent to Egypt, working as an Army Co-operation Unit. The Squadron went on to fly the Lysander, Hurricane and Spitfire throughout World War II in the Middle East.

In 1956 the Squadron was based at Malta, flying the Meteor FR Mk 9 which were operated until 1958 when the unit once again disbanded. Reforming at RAF Tangmere in 1958 the Squadron was equipped with the Hunter F Mk 6. Markings were now applied to the sides of the fuselage consisting of Light Blue and Yellow rectangles, with Yellow aircraft letters on the tails and repeated in Black on the nosewheel door. The Squadron Commander's aircraft was serialed XG168 and bore White wing tips with the initials G W in Yellow outlined in Black on the aircraft's tail. During March of 1958, the unit was posted to Nicosia, Cyprus and shortly after, to Akrotiri where it remained until disbanding in 1959.

Reformed once again at Eastleigh, Nairobi within the same year, the squadron took over 142 Squadron's Venom FB Mk 4s. The Venom was operated for only a year when the unit returned to the United Kingdom to RAF Stradishall, where it received the Hunter FGA Mk 9 during 1960. A few months later the squadron moved back to Eastleigh, and then moved to Khormaksar in 1961. The fuselage rectangles were raised to a point level with the top of the roundels, and on some aircraft the wing tips were painted white (Yellow on others). The aircraft letters were Yellow and Black. During the late 1960s the markings were moved from the fuselage to the side of the Hunter's nose, however, the markings were considerably smaller and now in the shape of an arrowhead with a Sphinx emblem superimposed on the arrow. The Hunter served with the Squadron until it disbanded in 1971.

Hawker Hunters known to be on strength with No 208 Squadron
F Mk 6 - XE579 (A), XE556 (B), XE599 (C), XF441 (D), XG1658 (G W)
XF428 (S)
FGA Mk 9 - XG134 (A), XJ687 (B), XK140 (H), XF421 (H), XJ691 (G)
XK139 (J), XG205 (K)

NO 234 SQUADRON

No 234 Squadron was formed as a Flying Boat unit in August of 1918 and disbanded in 1919. Reformed as a Fighter Squadron during 1939 and equipped with Blenheims, by July of 1940 the unit was flying Spitfire Mk Is in Cornwall, and flew various marks of the Spitfire until 1945 when the Mustang Mk III came into use for long range Bomber Escort Duties. During the autumn of 1946 the Squadron disbanded.

Reformed in Germany during August of 1952, it flew the Vampire FB Mk 5 and FB Mk 9. The Venom was operated until 1954 when it was replaced by the Sabre F Mk 1 at Geilenkirchen. The Sabres carried the Squadron's Black rectangles with Red diamonds flanking the roundels.

However, in June of 1956, when the Hunter F Mk 4s arrived, with the rectangles being re-positioned to the nose with a Black Griffon in the center. White aircraft letters were applied to the tails, and repeated in Red on the nose wheel doors. No 234 Squadron remained at Geilenkirchen until disbanding in 1957.

No 234 Squadron was again reformed late in 1958, this time as a training unit under No 229 OCU at RAF Chivenor, and being re-numbered from a Reserve Squadron already in existence at the Station. No 234 was again equipped with the Hunter F Mk 4 and retained their distinctive Squadron markings except that the Griffon was now centered on a White disc. The Hunters carried White 'ES' code letters at the base of the tails with White individual aircraft numbers painted on the top of the tails, and repeated in Black on the nosewheel doors. The wing tips were also painted White.

During 1961 the Hunter F Mk 6 replaced the F Mk 4, and while retaining essentially the same Squadron markings, they also carried White tails and spines for a while. However, full camouflage soon returned to these aircraft, and by 1968 the individual aircraft number was painted Black on to a Yellow disc, repeated in Black on a Yellow nosewheel door.

The Hunters served with No 234 Squadron at Chivenor until 1974, when 229 OCU transferred to RAF Brawdy in Wales and then served along side the Hawk T Mk 1s.

Hawker Hunters known to be on strength with No 234 Squadron
F Mk 1 - WT575 (RS) A, WT642 (RS) C, WT630 (RS) J, WT624 (RS) M
WT631 (RS) N, WT635 (RS) O, WT651 (RS) Q, WT688 (RS) U
WT697 (RS) Z, WW606 (RS) H, WW608 (ES) E, WW634 (RS) F   WW644 (RS) Y
F Mk 4 - XF991 (A), XF943 (A), WV363 (K), XF293 (N), WV332 (P), WT737 (ES) B,
WT795 (ES) O, WV394 (RS) 3, WW648 (ES) J, WW658 (RS) 5, XE675 (RS) 7
Mk 6 - XE591 (8), XE656 (20), XF386 (33), XG131 (41), XF443 (51)
XL577 (82) T Mk 7 - XL617 (95), XL618 (87)
FGA Mk 9 - XF456 (S), XG151 (H), XG260 (T)
FR Mk 10 - WW594 (11), XE596 (13), XE626 (9), XF426(12)

(Below) F Mk 6, XG170 (52), carries No 234 Squadron's griffen on a White circle between rectangles Black containing two rows of Red diamonds while assigned to 229 OCU. 1968 (Map).

(Above) FR Mk 10, XF426 (12), of 229 OCU with a White spine, which was carried by this training unit for only a short time. RAF Chivenor, 1965 (Map).

(Below) T Mk 7, XL577 (82), of No 234 Squadron in overall Silver with Day-glo stripes on the nose and rear fuselage. (Map)

(Above) F4 WT771 (C) of 222 Squadron at the end of its life but still carrying its Red and Blue Squadron checkers. (Map)

NO 222 SQUADRON

No 222 Squadron was formed on 1 April 1918 carrying out a general duties role in Greece. After about a year of operations No 222 Squadron disbanded in 1919.

Reforming at RAF Duxford in 1939, the squadron trained on Blenheims before re-equipping as a Fighter Squadron on Spitfire Mk Is in 1940. From 1941 to 1945 the Squadron flew various marks of the Spitfire, converting to the Tempest in 1945. Based at RAF Tangmere in 1947, flying the Gloster Meteor F Mk 4, it re-equipped with the Meteor F Mk 8 while based at Leuchars, Scotland in 1950.

During 1954 the Meteors were being replaced by Hunter F Mk 1s and Squadron colors began to appear on the fuselage sides consisting of Red and Blue checkered rectangles. Individual aircraft letters were applied in White at the rear of the fuselage, and repeated in Red on the nosewheel door.

The Hunter F Mk 4 replaced the F Mk 1 in August of 1956 with markings remaining the same except that the checkers were raised level with the top of the roundel. The aircraft letter was moved from the fuselage to the sides of the tail. The Hunter was the last Fighter to serve with the Squadron, being disbanded at Leuchars late in 1957.

Hawker Hunters known to have been on strength with No 222 Squadron
F Mk 1 - WT619 (B), WT651 (C), WT637 (G), WT630 (T)
F Mk 4 - WT771 (C), WV386 (G), WW650 (R), WV327 (U), XE678 (X),
WV399 (B), WT811 (D), WT710 (QW), WT721 (B)

NO 245 SQUADRON

Formed in 1917 and equipped with the Short 260, No 245 Squadron carried out anti-submarine duties during World War I and was disbanded in 1919 at Fishguard.

The Squadron reformed in October of 1939 as a Fighter unit, flying various marks of the Hurricane until 1943 when the Typhoon came into use in the fighter/bomber role and Ranger duties.

After the war, the Squadron was equipped with the Meteor F Mk 3, Meteor F Mk 4, and the Meteor F Mk 8 until April of 1957. The F Mk 8 variant was used for in-flight refuelling experiments while still an operational unit, taking fuel from USAF B-29 Superfortresses. The Meteors were initially overall Silver, but were later camouflaged, carrying Blue and Yellow checkers in rectangles on either side of the roundels.

When the Squadron received the Hunter F Mk 4 during the spring of 1957 the checkers were reduced in size and moved to the sides of the nose. A yellow aircraft letter was carried on the aircraft's tail and is believed have been repeated in Black on the nose wheel door. The Hunter had served with the Squadron for only four months, when the unit disbanded at RAF Stradishall in July of 1957.

Hawker Hunters known to have been on strength with No 245 Squadron
F Mk 4 - WV330 (D), XE687 (G), XE686 (Q)

NO 233 OCU

Mention should be made of No 233 OCU based at RAF Pembrey in Wales. In 1957 this Unit was operating Hunter F Mk 1s. No special markings, colors, or emblems were carried. However, the Hunters carried a Yellow code letter on the fuselage sides between the roundel and serial number. Yellow wing tips were also carried. 233 OCU continued to serve at RAF Wittering with later marks of Hunters until becoming the Harrier conversion unit.

Hawker Hunters known to be on strength with 233 Operational Conversion Unit
WT615 (A), WW609 (B), WT634 (C), WT620 (D), WW604 (F), WT638 (G)
WT643 (J), WT695 (N), WT657 (O), WT578 (S), WT613 (U), WT576 (V)

(Above) F Mk 4, WV 317 (S), of No 247 Squadron during an Armed Forces day display. The rectangles were Red with Black outlines.

NO 247 SQUADRON

No 247 Squadron was formed in 1917 at RNAS Felixtow to carry out anti-submarine patrol duties flying Sopwith Seaplanes. The unit was disbanded in 1919.

Reformed as a Fighter unit in 1940, the Hawker Hurricane was flown from December of 1940 until early 1943 when it re-equipped with the Typhoon in the fighter attack and Bomber roles.

No 247 was based at Odiham in 1946 when it received its first jet Fighters, the Vampire F Mk 1 which was flown in various marks until early 1951 when the Meteor F Mk 8 was received. Red rectangles had been carried in a small format on the Vampire FB Mk 5 and in a larger format on the fuselage sides of the Meteor.

The squadron got the Hunter F Mk 1 in June of 1955 which are believed have been used as a conversion aircraft during the weeks prior to the delivery of the Hunter F Mk 4s in July 1955. The Hunter F Mk 4 bore Red rectangles flanking the fuselage roundels essentially similar to the Vampires. A Yellow or White aircraft letter was positioned on the sides of the tail and repeated in Red on Silver nosewheel doors.

During the spring of 1957 the F Mk 4 was replaced by the Hunter F Mk 6 variant, with the markings remaining the same. However, the Squadron Commander's aircraft, serialed XF454, bore a Yellow question mark on a Red tail. During exercise Vigilant in May of 1957, the defending squadrons applied White paint to their aircraft in varying styles. However, 247 Squadron painted both the tail and spine of their Hunters in White.

The Hunter F Mk 6 was the last aircraft to serving with the Squadron when it disbanded at Odiham in 1957.

Hawker Hunters known to have been on strength with No 247 Squadron
F Mk 1 - WW638 (J)
F Mk 4 - WT795 (A), WW254 (C), WT775 (Q), XF320 (R), WV317 (S)
WT810 (W), XE662 (Z)
F Mk 6 - XF437 (A), XF455 (B), XF454 (?), XE581 (T), XF424 (V) XF442 (Z)

(Above) F Mk 2, WN898 (A), of No 257 Squadron on display during Bentwater's Armed Forces day display in 1955. The squadron rectangles were Green and Yellow checkers. (M.Olmsted).

(Above) This impeccable Hunter F Mk 5, WP189, was the aircraft assigned to the Wattisham Wing Leader, and flown along-side the F Mk 2s of 257 Squadron, and F Mk 5s of No 263 Squadron, the two squadrons of the Wattisham Wing. The Wattisham Station crest is carried on the nose, and the Wing Commander's pennant is painted below the cockpit and on the nosewheel door. (C.C.H. Cole)

NO 257 SQUADRON

No 257 was formed in 1914 at RNAS Dundee as an anti-submarine Reconnaissance unit flying Sopwith Seaplanes. It disbanded in June of 1919.

Reformed in May of 1940 as a Fighter Squadron flying the Spitfire I, by June of 1940 it was flying the Hurricane, which it would fly until 1942 when the squadron was re-equipped with the Hawker Typhoon. The Typhoon was flown until 1945 when the Squadron disbanded.

Reformed at RAF Church Fenton in 1946, 257 Squadron flew the Meteor F Mk 3 for the next two years, re-equipping with the F Mk 4 in 1948, which it flew until 1950. During this period the Meteors carried code letters flanking the fuselage roundels, but with the introduction of the F Mk 8, Green and Yellow checkers were added to the roundels.

No 257 Squadron was the first unit to receive the Hunter F Mk 2, when it replaced the Meteors at RAF Wattisham in November of 1954. The Hunters were soon marked with the Squadron's Green and Yellow checkers applied in a rectangle to the fuselage sides. The aircraft letter was Yellow outlined in Green and applied to the sides of the tail with a Green letter being applied to a Yellow nosewheel door.

Like other Hunter units the squadron markings were moved to the sides of the nose, with the Squadron's Chinthe emblem placed in the center. The Hunter served with the squadron until it disbanded at RAF Wattisham in early 1957.

Hawker Hunters known to have been on strength with No 257 Squadron
F Mk 2 - WN898 (A), WN903 (B), WN953 (C), WN917 (E), WN950 (F), WN907 (H)
WN943 (M), WN904 (Q), WN948 (R), WN915 (T), WN914 (V), WN918 (W)

(Below) F Mk 5, WP108 (RA), of 263 Squadron. This was the personal aircraft of Squadron Leader R. Aytoun, No 263 Squadron's Commander. RAF Wattisham, 1955/56 (R.Abbott)

NO 263 SQUADRON

No 263 was formed as a Coastal Reconnaissance unit in 1918 equipped with the Sopwith Seaplane, and was active for just over a year when the unit disbanded in May of 1919.

Reforming in October of 1938, the unit became a Fighter Squadron equipped with the Gladiator as its first aircraft, but in June of 1940 the squadron received the Hurricane. The Westland Whirlwind began to equip the unit in mid 1940, being used for convoy patrols, attacks on airfields, and intercepting bomber attacks until it was replaced by the Hawker Typhoon in December of 1943.

After the war 263 Squadron was disbanded, but was quickly reformed in September of 1945, moving to RAF Church Fenton with Meteor F Mk 3s, and later to Horsham St Faith with the Meteor F Mk 4 variant. Squadron markings were introduced on the fuselage sides of the Meteor F Mk 4, consisting of Red rectangles with Blue crosses superimposed. These markings were perpetuated on the Meteor F Mk 8 with which the Squadron was equipped when it moved to RAF Wattisham in 1950.

In January of 1955 the Hunter F Mk 2 joined 263 Squadron and the squadron markings were moved to the sides of the aircraft's nose with the Red rectangles now flanking a Lion emblem. A Red aircraft letter outlined in Yellow was applied to the tail and was repeated on the Silver nosewheel door. The next Hunter variant to serve with the unit was the F Mk 5, with the markings remaining essentially the same with the exception of the addition of a thin Yellow outline on the outside of the rectangles. The Squadron Commander's aircraft (WP108) carried his initials 'RA' and a Red lightning bolt on the tail, all with Yellow outlines.

Both variants of the Hunter served until October of 1957 when it was superseded by the Hunter F Mk 6. Again the markings remained the same, with the addition of White wing tips. The Squadron, which moved to, and remained at RAF Stradishall, until its disbanding in July of 1958.

Hawker Hunters known to have been on strength with No 263 Squadron
F Mk 2 - WN915, WN921 (S), WN944 (H), WN947 (R), WN900 (U), WN946 (N)
F Mk 5 - WN985, WN990 (F), WP107 (G), WP108 (RA), WP189, WN981 (V) WN983 (D), WN976 (B)
F Mk 6 - XE615 (A), XE607, XE626 (P), XE584 (W)

(Below) Hawker Hunter, XE584 (W), of 263 Squadron with the Red rectangles and Blue nose crosses, and White wingtips. Shepard's Grove, 17 May 1958.

CENTRAL FIGHTER ESTABLISHMENT

RAF West Raynham was the home of the Central Fighter Establishment containing a number of specialist squadrons: **AFDS - Air Fighting Development Squadron. DFCS - Day Fighter Combat School. DFLS - Day Fighter Leaders School.** The Air Fighting Development Squadron was formed at RAF Northolt on 20 October 1934, under the auspices of the Air Fighting Development Establishment (AFDE). Information as to the units work during the early years is somewhat sketchy, but the main tasks at its formation were the study of tactics and methods of attack of single-seat Fighters against enemy bombers and formations, the arrangement and design of Armament Equipment, and the general design lay-out and performance of aircraft. During 1938, affiliation exercises were carried out with Bomber Squadrons. Lectures were also regularly provided for members of the RAF Staff College.

Affiliation exercises were flown again during 1939 with Bomber Command Wellingtons, Hampdens and Whitleys. A detachment of the 1st Anti-Aircraft Battery, Royal Engineers was also attached to the unit for co-operation in AFDE night flying trials. In October of 1939 the first of a series of two day fighting courses was begun.

On 16 December 1940 AFDE moved to RAF Duxford, where the name of the unit was changed to Air Fighting Development Unit (AFDU). During January and February of 1941 AFDU carried out special trials with fighters and gliders. Throughout World War II AFDU carried out tactical trials to test the fighting capabilities of nearly every aircraft it could get its hands on, including re-conditioned enemy aircraft (the JU 88, FW 190 and Bf 109). New air armament equipment and camouflage were tested, developed and improved. Courses in the use of the cannon, the cine-camera gun, and fighting tactics were undertaken. Films on the various aspects of the unit's work were made and shown to other units of the RAF. Detachments from various units visited AFDU to see and learn the latest information on air fighting. There was no aspect of air fighting, offensive or defensive, which the unit did not test, develop or improve.

(Below) Hunter F Mk 6, XG192 (F), of the Fighter Combat School in Day-glo markings. 1960. (Map).

On 25 March 1943 AFDU moved to RAF Wittering. On 18 June 1944 one of the earliest of the enemy V-1 Flying Bombs (Buzz Bombs) was destroyed by a pilot of FFDU. Pieces of the exploding bomb penetrated the Hawker Tempest he was flying, but a safe landing was made. The AFDU was disbanded on 26 October 1944, and reformed the same day as the Air Fighting Development Squadron (AFDS). The squadron's first task was trials of dropping fire bombs from Hawker Typhoons aircraft. Tests and trials were also continued with the Messerschmitt Bf 109G and BF 110.

In December of 1944 the Squadron moved to RAF Tangmere, where the Fighter Leaders School of the Central Fighter Establishment (CFE) was formed. During September of 1945 CFE moved to RAF West Raynham.

In 1955 Hunters were being used by the Central Fighter Establishment. AFDS aircraft lacked any special markings, although it is believed that nosewheel doors carried the last three digits of the serial number painted on the top of the door. Hunter XK149 had a Red nosewheel door with '149' painted diagonally across it in white.

In 1962 CFE moved to RAF Binbrook, remaining there until disbanding on 1 February 1966.

Day Fighter Leaders School

In 1955 the Day Fighter Leaders School (DFLS), was operating the Hunter F Mk 1. The squadron was divided into two flights, each with its own distinctive colors. 'A' Flight had the spines of their Hunters painted Red, with Red wing and tailplane bands. 'B' Flight carried the same scheme but in Yellow. The paint on the aircraft's spine ran from the cockpit to the leading edge of the tail, tapering off at the Black di-electric panel. In some cases nose wheel doors were painted in the appropriate color with the serial number painted in White diagonally across it. By the end of 1956, the whole tail including the tailplanes were painted in the flight colors.

By the time the Hunter F Mk 6 was delivered, the Day Fighter Leaders School had been renamed the Fighter Combat School, which was now painted in White on the noses of the aircraft, below and just forward of the cockpit area. One or two aircraft also carried a small Central Fighter Establishment crest just above the title.

From 1961, both 'A' and 'B' flights were re-painted in a Dayglo Orange scheme as previously described. It is possible that one flight may well have adopted a flourescent light green scheme. Aircraft code letters were painted Black on the tail and on the nosewheel door, however, there were one or two exceptions with White letters being carried. The summer of 1963 saw miniature 63 (shadow) Squadron markings applied, replacing the 'Fighter Combat School' title.

Hawker Hunters known to have on strength with The Fighter Combat School
F Mk 6 - XG197 (A), XG204 (B), XG209 (C), XG206 (E), XF450 (D), XG514 (F) XG192 (F), XF382 (R), XF512 (S), XF418 (T), XF453 (V)

(Above) Hunter F Mk 6, XG197 (A), a small No 63 squadron emblem is painted on the nose. 1963/64 (Map).